THE
END
OF
CHEAP
CHINA

THE
END
OF
CHEAP
CHINA

ECONOMIC AND CULTURAL TRENDS
THAT WILL **DISRUPT THE WORLD**

SHAUN REIN

WILEY

John Wiley & Sons, Inc.

Published by John Wiley & Sons, Inc., Hoboken, New Jersey.
Published simultaneously in Canada.

For general information on our other products and services or for technical support, please contact our Customer Care Department within the United States at (800) 762-2974, outside the United States at (317) 572-3993 or fax (317) 572-4002.

Wiley publishes in a variety of print and electronic formats and by print-on-demand. Some material included with standard print versions of this book may not be included in ebooks or in print-on-demand. If this book refers to media such as a CD or DVD that is not included in the version you purchased, you may download this material at http://booksupport.wiley.com. For more information about Wiley products, visit www.wiley.com.

Library of Congress Cataloging-in-Publication Data:

Rein, Shaun, 1977-
  The end of cheap China : economic and cultural trends that will disrupt the world /Shaun Rein.
      pages cm
   ISBN 978-1-118-17206-3 (cloth); ISBN 978-1-118-22786-2 (ebk);
   ISBN 978-1-118-23994-0 (ebk); 978-1-118-26455-3 (ebk)
        1. China—Economic conditions—21st century. 2. China—Social conditions—21st century. 3. China—Commerce. 4. Labor—China. 5. Costs, Industrial—China. 6. Consumption (Economics)—China.   I. Title.
   HC427.95.R447 2012
   330.951—dc23
                                                                           2011045221

Printed in the United States of America

10 9 8 7 6 5 4 3 2

Tom Tom,
May life bring you many bright lights.
Love, Ba Ba

CONTENTS

The year was 1998. Steve Jobs was years away from introducing the iPod to the world, and audiences were packing cinemas across the globe to see Leonardo DiCaprio's love affair with Kate Winslet in *Titanic*.

I turned off the lights in my grubby hotel room in Changchun, a dingy industrial city in northeast China famous for being the capital of Manchukuo, the Japanese-controlled puppet state during World War II. I had been sitting upright on a hard, wooden train seat for 18 hours all the way from Tianjin, and my back ached. The room's air conditioner unit wheezed loudly, and a potent mixture of smells emanated from the bathroom, but I was so exhausted I started to drift off to sleep anyway.

Then the calls started.

The first time I answered, a giggly, cutesy voice on the other end playfully asked, "Do you want some fun?" I knew what "fun" meant. No, I told the voice, not my style, and I hung up. Undeterred, the girlish voice kept calling back every five minutes. "Do you want some comfort?" she cooed. I hung up. The phone rang again. "Do you have any aches I can massage away?"

I fumbled around in the dark trying to disconnect the phone, without success. Finally I ripped the phone out of the socket. It was damaged, but I figured I'd just settle up with the hotel manager the next day—after all, everything in China then was cheap.

Then there was a knock on the door. I opened it, and standing in front of me was an absolutely stunning girl. She had a slender, lithesome body, mesmerizing coal-black eyes, and a perky nose. Her hair flowed in dark waves to her shoulders, and she wore a deep-blue cocktail dress that hinted amply at what was underneath but didn't reveal too much. A fruity perfume scent hung in the air around her. I remember thinking how gorgeous she was. She easily could have been a cover model for a fashion magazine, maybe *Teen Vogue*.

She smiled. "Twenty dollars," she said, and mimed with her hand and mouth what that amount would buy me. Then she told me what 25 bucks would get. I stared at her blankly for a few moments, sweat beading up on my palms and brow, finally said no, and crawled back to bed alone. Seemingly as soon as I started to drift off again, the knocks started again. It was the start of a long, lonely, sleepless night.

When I first arrived in China in the mid-1990s to study Chinese at Nankai University, gorgeous young prostitutes like the one that stood at my door in Changchun that night were everywhere. They were in hotels, saunas, karaoke bars, even coffee shops. They would sit, elegantly, waiting for traveling businessmen—mostly middle-aged white foreigners with bulging guts—and saunter over to them to make their pitch for a little "comfort." They were easy to spot because, unlike most of the rest of the population that dressed in conservative matronly old clothes, they carried Motorola mobile phones and Louis Vuitton bags. What amazed me was that practically all of them were dazzlingly beautiful.

Now, 15 years later, as the founder of China Market Research Group (CMR), a market research firm that helps companies as varied as Apple, Kentucky Fried Chicken, Richemont, LG Electronics, and DuPont develop their strategies for China, I have witnessed a total turnaround in the labor pool and how people dress and eat.

No longer do you find gorgeous prostitutes everywhere. On a trip to Beijing in 2011, I stayed at one of the ritziest hotels in the capital. Glancing around the lobby, I could still spot the hookers easily enough, only now they were middle aged and ugly. They wore too much makeup and had paunches like many of the aging Western businessmen they serviced. As I stood in the elevator on the way up to my room, I realized I couldn't remember the last time I'd received a call at night in a hotel room, and that it was becoming rare to even be approached by a hooker. What had happened?

The explanation is simple enough. In the mid-1990s, job opportunities were scarce in China, so even the most beautiful young girls were desperate enough to work as prostitutes, selling their bodies to feed themselves and send money home to their families in the countryside. But China's economy and job market have seen dramatic changes in the past decade and a half. As more attractive, better-paying job opportunities increased, pretty young girls took advantage of better options, and the pool of prostitutes got uglier as a result. The uglification of Chinese prostitutes is part of a broader trend that is the subject of this book, *The End of Cheap China*.

Many Americans have an idea of China as possessing a limitless supply of cheap labor. It is easy to understand why. From the data points most readily available to the average American—the ubiquitous "Made in China" tag on products filling the shelves at Walmart and Target, and China's world's-largest, 1.3-billion-strong population—it is quite natural to conclude that there must be swarms of Chinese ready to jump onto a factory floor and make more products for Americans to consume.

But despite China's massive population, jobs are now abundant, and gender equality in general is improving. In fact, one of the biggest obstacles that companies operating in that nation now face is the lack of available workers—there are more job openings than employable workers in many cases. Huge foreign investment has resulted in the creation of millions of new jobs, and because of the one-child policy, when workers retire there are fewer and fewer young people to replace them in the labor force.

There has also been a shift in the mentality of Chinese workers from even a decade ago, when good jobs were hard to come by and people would accept harsh conditions if it meant having a steady job, a roof over the head, and food to eat. The younger generation's optimism about their futures and career prospects is palpable. They have witnessed China's rise to economic superpower status, come through the financial crisis stronger than any other nation, and have yet to live through a downturn.

Filled with electric optimism, and seeing opportunities to get rich everywhere, they are no longer willing to debase themselves in humiliating work, slave away in factories thousands of miles away from homes and families, or toil in jobs that do not empower them to achieve their white-collar dreams. In turn, they have started to buy the products that they used to make, making the Chinese consumer growth story one of the most exciting and important for the next decade. It is an opportunity for companies trying to offset dwindling growth in the developed world, and poses problems for policy makers who need to deal with inflationary pressures as Chinese people eat more meat, buy more cars and air conditioners, and live in larger homes.

Using interviews with billionaires, government officials, executives of Chinese and foreign firms, poor migrant workers, and even prostitutes, I will explain the larger phenomenon of why Chinese workers are no longer willing to slave away for cheap wages to assemble Apple iPhones and Nike Air Zooms and what that means for the rest of the world. China's evaporating cheap-labor pool will disrupt supply chains and consumption habits around the world. Executives and policy makers need to prepare to be ahead of the curve, to evolve and take advantage of the changes—or else face extinction.

Companies can no longer manufacture cheaply in China, and may need to rethink their strategies and shift manufacturing to lower-cost production centers like Vietnam or Indonesia—or even back to the United States in some cases. As thousands of factories in China have already done, they might have to automate production lines and produce higher-value goods, or face the prospect of shutting down completely if margins are squeezed too tightly. Only one thing is for certain: Rising labor, real estate, and commodities costs in China will cause prices for everyday Americans to rise and crimp our consumption-oriented way of life.

I will further examine the political and sociological reasons why Chinese incomes are soaring so fast, how that is affecting domestic Chinese consumption, and what that means for businesses. Instead of the market to produce *in*, China has become the market to sell *into*. Although famous for making Nike shoes, China is now Nike's second-largest market in the world, generating $2.1 billion in revenue in 2011 and boasting Nike's fattest margins anywhere in the world. Nike expects to double sales there by 2015. In 2010, China became the largest market for autos with over 17 million sold. It has become Buick's largest market after the Detroit carmaker reinvented itself as a must-have brand for rising Chinese executives, and there are half-year waits to buy Porsches. Yum! Brands, the parent company of Kentucky Fried Chicken, generates over 40 percent of its global revenue in China, and hour-long lines to get into Pizza Hut are a common sight at the malls sprouting up across the country. Chinese people are the second-largest buyers of luxury products, buying $15.6 billion worth in 2011. China has become the must-win market for consumer product companies.

Finally, I will show how rising consumption by China's 350-million-strong middle class—who all want homes, air conditioners, cars, and a piece of the good life—will strain commodities markets around the world, further adding to inflationary pressures. Their increasing demand will cause inevitable tensions as Chinese investment expands into other countries and continents like Australia, Canada, and Africa to secure access to limited natural resources. China's demand for commodities will further disrupt the international status quo as the Chinese government cements deals with countries like Iran and South Sudan that are viewed as unsavory and often have divergent interests from the United States.

As America adjusts to having a true rival economic superpower for the first time since the end of the Cold War, it is critical for the world to understand what China was, what it is now, and what it could become in the coming decades. Too often the rise of a new power, combined with a weak global economy, creates conditions disposed to military movement. The first half of the twentieth century devastated the world and left tens of millions dead and hundreds of millions displaced, as Germany, the United Kingdom, the Soviet Union, Japan, and the United States competed over a new world order in the face of weak economic growth and limited access to natural resources.

Rarely do major shifts in global power go smoothly, as many predict will happen with America and China. One must know history and never forget it. Yet outright conflict is not inevitable between the world's two superpowers, and the world now has better global institutions in place for arbitration, like the World Trade Organization and the United Nations. China also has a different culture, one less based on missionary zeal than those of many traditionally Christian nations like the United States and the United Kingdom that might make it less likely to wage ideological and military battles far beyond its own borders.

Fear mongering, misinformation, and hysterics about China's rise are hitting the American airwaves on a daily basis, clouding rational discourse. Nobel Prize–winning economist and *New York Times* columnist Paul Krugman, and Senator Charles Schumer from New York, feed the flames of fear and anger by arguing that China is stealing American jobs by keeping its currency low, and that America should take an aggressive approach with it. Celebrity businessman, entertainer, and billionaire Donald Trump agrees, and thinks America should slap a 25 percent tariff on all Chinese imports. President George W. Bush's former counterterrorism and cybersecurity advisor Richard Clarke argues that America needs to beef up its cyber warfare capabilities, because it is under daily attack by Chinese assaults that could threaten America's security just as much as conventional weapons.

Rising anti-China rhetoric is gaining currency and is dangerous and misguided—the last thing anyone needs is the world's two superpowers in conflict, and strong rhetoric has a way of being self-fulfilling. In a study run by Professor Orville Schell, the nonprofit, New York–based Asia Society estimated that America could lose up to $2 trillion in Chinese investment due to anti-China hysteria, as Chinese firms look to Europe, South

America, Africa, and other investment climes more welcoming to Chinese money.

More urgently, factions with chips on their shoulders within China don't want to be pushed around by America anymore. They are demanding a more muscular Chinese military presence that is willing to flex its muscles to demonstrate to its neighbors and the rest of the world there is an end to American hegemony and a new world order. In 2011 China launched stealth airplanes and an aircraft carrier, and took a more aggressive and nationalistic stance in disputes with Japan and in the South China Sea with the Philippines and Vietnam. Although China historically does not have a history of straying far beyond its borders in military exercises, preferring to stay closer to its orbit, a meek, inwardly focused China is not a foregone conclusion as threats to its stability from internal issues diminish while threats from the outside rise.

It does not matter if you are a businessman, politician, teacher, student, or just someone curious about China and changes in the world today: It is important to understand, by using objective data points rather than red herrings and phantom facts, how the End of Cheap China will impact all our lives. I aim to do just that by tracking my own experiences in China, from my time as a teenager in the mid-1990s until now as an entrepreneur and consultant, and how I came to learn about and understand the country.

1

CHINESE BILLIONAIRES OUTNUMBER AMERICAN ONES

I was sitting on a leather couch in an opulent meeting room in Shanghai's five-star Okura Garden Hotel in the former French Concession in 2010. Above my head dangled a chandelier of such scale that it would fit in at Versailles. I imagined former supreme leader Mao Zedong sitting in the room, as he did decades earlier when the hotel was his stomping ground on visits to Shanghai.

A man who appeared to be in his early forties stood in front of me, doing tai chi. He was thin, had a fully shaven head, and wore a simple white oxford shirt unbuttoned at the collar. There was a serene aura about him that commanded the respect of everyone else in a room that included some of the most successful businessmen in China; he seemed to be the king among kings. He smiled at me, asked me to sit, and gently requested that someone pour me some tea as he continued his routine.

Looking around, most of the others joining us were worth tens if not hundreds of millions of dollars. A few might have crossed the billion-dollar mark. All were entrepreneurs who had built up brands every Chinese person knows. There was Chen He Lin, the slight and gregarious founder of ASD, a kitchenware company known by Chinese housewives for durable and safe but affordable crockery. He had looked at me curiously, perhaps because I was the youngest and the only foreigner in the room, or perhaps because I was the only face he didn't recognize. After looking me up and down, he too grinned at me and handed me his business card.

Sitting to my right was a tall, bald man chain-smoking furiously. He stuck out because he was dressed in an all-white athletic suit while everyone else was wearing dress clothes. Like the king of the room, he too had a shaved head, although unlike his friend he did not offer me his card. He pretty much ignored me when I asked him a question about his business. He told me his name was Shi Yuzhu. He was famous for losing his entire fortune before building it back up again when he took his online game company, Giant Interactive, public on the New York Stock Exchange. Shi Yuzhu became infamous several months later among Western investors for ultra nationalism when he publicly sided with Alibaba's founder, Jack Ma, in his public dispute with Yahoo! over the ownership of the online payment service Alipay by calling Ma on his Sina microblog a "patriotic hooligan."

On Shi Yuzhu's right side sat Zhou Xin, a towering man with short-cropped hair who reminded me of Yogi Bear. He was the cofounder of E-House, an online and offline real estate brokerage firm that was also publicly traded on the New York Stock Exchange. He beamed at me with a mix of pride and humility when I told him that consumers my firm had interviewed had responded they were very happy with his company's products and services.

While the rest of us listened, the man doing tai chi started to talk about the business environment and the economic problems facing the country due to the financial crisis in America and Europe. The man's name was Guo Guangchang, the founder of the Fosun Group. *The Hurun Report*, which tracks the net worth of the Chinese rich, estimates Guo's wealth at nearly $5 billion.

As I listened to Guo and the others discuss the business climate, I looked around the room at their faces. All seemed to have the intensity of Olympic athletes about to compete. Optimism and confidence, born from being raised with nothing but making it big through their own sweat and grit, seemed to ooze from their pores. They knew they could overcome any challenges with enough hard work and patience.

To my left a number of the executives gathered to talk about joining forces to lobby the government more. They were worried about a credit crunch hitting small and medium enterprises, and they wanted to join together to present their case to the government to remedy the situation. Concerns about underground banks, loan sharks really, calling in loans was starting to become a topic of conversation.

Listening to the discussion, it was clear these were some of the savviest businessmen not just in China but in the world. I have advised chief executives of Fortune 500 firms and trailblazing entrepreneurs whose innovations change the world, but these Chinese entrepreneurs were as impressive as any executive or thinker I had ever met, and perhaps even more so, considering the filthy poverty and chaos they had grown up in just a few decades before.

Despite intellectual property problems, uneven government regulation, corruption, poorly trained labor forces, and difficulty raising capital, these battle-hardened executives had all taken risks and built up groundbreaking organizations in the last 10 years. It was also clear that these entrepreneurs were building up strong Chinese brands. None of them was simply copying Western business models or stealing intellectual property as many Westerners think all Chinese do—they were creating new ones.

Not only were these businessmen building brands in China, but many of them were also growing abroad organically and competing on foreign turf. Some had even begun buying up iconic foreign brands. Guo's Fosun Group had started scooping up stakes in foreign firms. He had acquired 7.1 percent of Club Med, the French resort company known for opening all-inclusive resorts in exotic locales, to cater to more of the 50 million Chinese tourists who travel abroad every year. Guo had also bought the rights to *Forbes* magazine in China, and had signed several major deals with foreign investment firms. His company had set up a $600 million joint investment fund with Prudential Financial to invest in foreign and Chinese firms that have significant growth potential in China. He had also launched a cobranded fund in renminbi (China's currency) with the politically well-connected Carlyle Group, the private equity firm that once had former President George H. W. Bush and British Prime Minister John Major on its payroll, for investment in China.

Looking at these executives, it became clear that too many Western observers of China foolishly discount the management and branding abilities of Chinese companies, much as many

American companies discounted Japanese firms like Toyota and Sony in the late 1970s. Aggressive, confident, and capital-rich Japanese firms quickly took advantage of bloated American firms like General Motors and painfully forced American companies to reassess their business models. Japanese firms went from making cheap, tacky products to defining quality in some industries. Chinese firms might similarly disrupt entire industries if American companies are not forward thinking enough to react to evolving Chinese companies and stay ahead in innovation before the business threat materializes.

When you walk along the aisles of your local Walmart or Best Buy, most products are marked with a "Made in China" label. Trying to keep costs down, many multinational companies established direct-owned manufacturing operations in China or began sourcing from Chinese-owned factories through intermediary firms like Li & Fung. Even in your own home, you would be hard pressed not to find at least some products in each room touting this sticker.

You would also probably be hard pressed to name any Chinese brands, despite China being the factory of the world for the last two decades and having the world's second-largest economy. Unless you had observed the rise of Chinese brands in the last decade, the absence of these brands in Walmart might lead you to agree with the many Western analysts who think that Chinese companies simply do not have the ability to build brands.

Atlantic Monthly journalist James Fallows is one of those observers. He calls the 44 percent of Americans who think China is the world's leading economic power, according to a 2009 Pew Center poll, "crazy" because he does not think

Americans can "name even 10 [brands] from China." Fallows continues, disparaging the research ability of Chinese scientists: "Name the most recent winner of a Nobel prize in science from a Chinese university or research institution." That was a trick question, because there have not been any winners.

Fallows believes Chinese companies cannot brand, and that its leading minds in the sciences do not have the innovation and creativity to win a Nobel Prize in the sciences. He seems to agree with the conventional wisdom of Western analysts that Chinese are better at copying what worked in America, building a clone of it, or simply ripping off intellectual property to make money. After all, many of China's publicly traded companies, such as search engine Baidu or e-commerce auction site Taobao, seem like rip-offs of Google and eBay. Are analysts like Fallows right, or are there deeper explanations why Americans cannot name many Chinese brands?

At first glance, Fallows is right. Few Americans would be able to name more than 10 Chinese brands. The ones Americans might know, like information and communications technology provider Huawei, tend to be more focused on selling products and services that are good enough but cheap to businesses. They tend to focus more on business-to-business clients, rather than on more fickle and brand-conscious end consumers. Or Americans might know brands like Huawei not because of their quality, but because of fears they are fronts for the Chinese military and pose security risks, which makes them a frequent target in the Western media and of members of Congress on the campaign trail. However, everyday Americans' lack of knowledge about Chinese brands does not really mean that Chinese companies cannot brand and build global champions. A deeper glance, and a basic understanding of recent Chinese history, will show that underestimating Chinese businesspeople as Fallows does would be foolish.

Not having a Nobel Prize winner in science does not mean Chinese scientists cannot conduct leading research. Such awards are usually conferred for work done decades earlier. Japanese scientists Ei-ichi Negishi and Akira Suzuki won the 2010 chemistry Nobel Prize for research conducted in the 1960s and 1970s—the same period when the Cultural Revolution was ravaging China, as we will explore in Chapter 3.

If Chinese scientists have not won a Nobel by 2050, one could then argue Chinese researchers in a Chinese institution cannot do groundbreaking research—but I bet one will. After all, when I was a graduate student at Harvard's Graduate School of Arts and Sciences at the turn of the millennium, more mainland Chinese were enrolled there than from any other country except America, and many of my classmates have been lured by government initiatives to recruit mainland scholars to return to Chinese universities rather than stay in America.

Fallows is also correct that few Americans know Chinese brands, but once again he is wrong about the reasons. He would be correct if it were still the 1990s, when Chinese management teams were weak and focused on the short term, but surprisingly, Fallows seems to have missed China's business evolution in the last decade.

Today's Chinese brands are quickly moving up the value chain to compete on branding and innovation rather than just on price. They have had to figure out earlier than foreign competitors how to deal with the End of Cheap China. Rising labor and real estate costs and demanding consumers are forcing them to think more long term about building sustainable brands and changing manufacturing operations, in order to command the fatter margins they need to stay alive.

Those entrepreneurs sitting with me at the Okura Garden Hotel are all developing strong brands—in fact, it is directly because of branding efforts that they have been able to beat local competitors over the past decade to emerge as domestic powers. They defeated state-owned enterprises, with their easy access to credit and political patronage, because they offered the market what it demanded and stayed ahead of trends. None had made their riches by being the stereotypical cheap Chinese original equipment manufacturer, squeezing razor-thin profits. They had created brands that had earned Chinese consumers' trust, and had become rich in the process.

A decade ago, most Chinese brands competed on price, but not because Chinese inherently lack creativity or the government stifles creativity and innovation. There are several reasons why executives' focus on planning was more short term.

First, incomes were still low. The dramatic, sustained rise in incomes and purchasing power that China has seen was only beginning, so it did not make sense to compete on anything but price. In the 1990s, China was steeped in real poverty. The average per capita gross domestic product (GDP) was less than $1,000 a year, and the majority of the country earned less than $300 a year, below the World Bank's definition of extreme poverty. Meat was often a luxury, and eating at a restaurant like McDonald's or KFC was reserved for special occasions. Hot showers were rare—most people still stood outside in full view of neighbors and passersby, using buckets to wash themselves, or went to company shower facilities on weekends. The lack of running water explains why even today getting your hair washed at a salon is an essential part of the hair-cutting process; in those days, visits to salons for a warm hair wash was a real treat.

Competing on anything other than price in that climate would have been foolish. Global brands took this strategy, launching global brands in China and investing for the long term. One Kodak executive told me in the 1990s they were investing not for short-term profits but to "make a lot of money twenty years from now." Fewer than 10 percent of Western brands selling into the Chinese market in the 1990s actually made money there, in part because no one could afford their products. Another reason was that Western brand positioning often did not fit the aspirations and needs of everyday Chinese people. It is hard to relate to Ralph Lauren, with its preppy lifestyle image of summering in the Hamptons, when you dream of indoor plumbing and eating meat for dinner.

The lack of profits and price sensitivity on consumers' part changed in less than a decade. In its 2010–2011 report, the U.S. Chamber of Commerce in Shanghai found that 78 percent of American companies now make money in China, and 87 percent reported revenue growth in 2010, up from 47 percent in 2009. A thriving middle class, with the desire and the money to sustain brands that focus on more than just price, is fueling these profits.

Brand managers must cater to the demands and sophistication of the market into which they are selling, and in China of the 1990s, levels of sophistication were pretty low. Few consumers had the money to buy real brands. It was natural that most Chinese companies and executive teams focused on maintaining low operating costs and sales channels to compete on price, when consumers could not afford to care about branding, and when labor and real estate costs were low enough to follow that strategy. Likewise, it is a natural progression that they are now evolving along with rising consumer sophistication to focus on building strong brands.

A second reason why brands did not emerge earlier is the importance of connections during the disruptive shift in the late 1990s toward encouraging private enterprise. Executives used governmental and other business connections to grab quick profits. It did not make sense to spend money and time building a brand when it was so easy to make gobs of fast money through these connections.

Well-connected executives could lobby the government to erect a building, get a lucrative supply contract, or buy assets that the government wanted to divest on the cheap. One son of a government official who became a real estate magnate and head of a large import-export firm told me that in the 1990s, local officials literally gave away land and sweetheart deals to well-connected people, in an effort to bring business and investment dollars to undeveloped areas because everyone was so poor.

In such market conditions, why would smart executives try to establish brands? It takes decades, huge budgets, and patience to build brands that resonate with consumers. Sony and Toyota took decades to gain a true foothold in the imaginations of American consumers as anything but cheap alternatives to American brands like General Electric and General Motors. Even Korean companies like Samsung and LG Electronics still lack the same premium brand positioning as Japanese firms, and are often seen as cheaper versions. Like Taiwanese brands such as phone maker HTC and computer maker Acer, they suffer from a perception of cheapness, even though their products rival the quality of any technology brand in the world.

Western businessmen in China still love to tell each other about the quasi-mystical importance of *guanxi,* which many define as "connections," when doing business with Chinese. But while good relationships are still important, as they are anywhere in the world, they do not have nearly the importance they once did, and are not nearly as vital as creating sustainable businesses that fit consumer needs and aspirations. Women don't buy lipstick because the owner of the brand is the son of some government official; they buy it because it makes them feel beautiful and vibrant. Nobody buys a shirt because a government official's wife owns the company, but because it fits body types and aspirations.

Even in real estate, where connections are often paramount, the government is now making land-leasing processes more transparent due to a renewed government focus on raising tax revenue and sustainable development. Domestic real estate developers like ShiMao Group, Vanke, and SOHO China are grabbing market share because their branding and style attracts Chinese home buyers more than because of connections. Many of the current political leaders' offspring are looking in Africa and other nations for investment, because it is easier to leverage connections in those markets than back at home, where quick moneymaking schemes are harder to come by.

Branding has become critical for Chinese firms as the combination of product safety scandals and increasing wealth has forced consumers to become sophisticated, skeptical, and less trusting. Well-branded firms that build trust with consumers are the ones grabbing market share and charging premiums for their products and services. Domestic firms like medical device company Mindray, herbal beverage maker Wang Lao Ji, dairy products company Mengniu Dairy, travel services firm CTRIP, and sports apparel firms Li Ning and Anta have emerged in the last decade as serious competitors to Western brands in China and even slowly abroad. These domestic firms understand this brand-oriented shift toward value in consumer demand. Retail sales have been growing 16 to 18 percent a year for the last five years. Mindray's competitor, General Electric X-Ray, even relocated its business unit to Beijing from Waukesha, Wisconsin, in 2011 because they expect China to be the fastest global growth market for medical devices.

Numerous domestic companies have already established their brands within Chinese consumers' minds, and are stepping into the global market. It would be shortsighted for Western brands to discount the abilities of domestic Chinese firms and their potential to compete globally, as observers such as Fallows do. To help lobby for its America-based initiatives and contracts, communications technology provider Huawei hired Amerilink Wireless, whose board includes retired U.S. Admiral William Owens, a former vice chairman of the Joint Chiefs of Staff; former U.S. House Majority Leader Richard Gephardt; and former World Bank President James Wolfensohn. Sports apparel maker Li Ning has set up design facilities near Nike's headquarters in Beaverton, Oregon.

One inevitable trend in the coming decades—now that rising costs and the end of easy money are forcing Chinese companies to become long-term strategic thinkers and look for new revenue models—is that more Chinese companies will go abroad. Western consumers had better get used to seeing Chinese brands, not just the "Made in China" stickers, on the shelves of America's retailers. Likewise, Western brands will have to start fending off competition from new emerging Chinese brands that will disrupt the world's markets and the global pecking order, much as Japanese firms did in the 1980s.

The consumer market has risen so fast in China that Chinese brands have focused for the most part on capturing the domestic market. My firm interviewed 500 senior executives with 100 of China's largest companies across 10 sectors during the financial crisis. Many executives told us they have not made much effort to become global players because the Chinese domestic market is growing so fast and the best opportunities are still at home, explaining in part why Americans have never heard of their brands. They also worry they do not have enough talent at the middle-management level to grow well abroad. They do not want lose long-term viability by making the same mistakes as Western brands when they first went into China, so they often move into markets like Africa, Southeast Asia, or Eastern Europe, where local competition is weak and stakes are not as high if they misstep. A new focus on the Western world is emerging; as companies get more ambitious, they create a professional middle-management layer, and the central government supports the rise of national champions through low-interest loans and tax breaks.

Many companies have started to invest abroad for future growth, too, as Guo Guangchang's Fosun Group has done. Over 70 percent of executives told us that they would take advantage of the financial crisis to accelerate their international expansion plans into America and Western Europe by capitalizing upon lower evaluations and cash-strapped competitors. They have been hiring leading advertising firms like Ogilvy & Mather and JWT to help shape their long-term positioning.

Branding is not an easy and short-term initiative. Chinese executives know this, so they often buy brands rather than building them. They have seen how long it took Sony, LG, and Samsung to become global players, and they do not want to wait so long. Instead of being second- or third-generation leaders, Chinese powerhouses still tend to be run by their founders, who made their success by conquering the impossible. Others run state-owned enterprises and are driven to make high-profile investments to help get promoted in the Communist Party ranks.

For example, under the stewardship of its founder, Li Shufu, auto manufacturer Geely bought the Swedish Volvo brand.

Home appliance giant Haier bought the domestic and and Southeast Asian operations of Japan's Sanyo. State-owned conglomerate Bright Food, China's second-largest food company, was rumored to have been in talks with Yoplait and nutritional supplement maker GNC before deals fell through, but it is still on the lookout for such megadeals. After buying Australian firm Manassen, Bright Food Chairman Wang Zongnan announced that he hopes 30 percent of its sales will come from overseas by 2016, and that he is actively looking to acquire more European or Australian companies in the food-distribution and sugar industries.

As I said good-bye to those leading entrepreneurs in the Okura Garden Hotel that night, it became very obvious that the rise of Chinese firms will disrupt world markets in a way most never could have imagined just a decade ago, and that the country was as far from Mao's vision of China as it could be. The End of Cheap China means that Western executives need to be prepared to fend off increased competition from their aggressive, battle-hardened, well-capitalized counterparts. Western consumers will get used to choosing products at Best Buy or Target with prominent Chinese brand names, or brands owned by Chinese investors, instead of just those bearing hidden "Made in China" stickers.

I was also left with some questions that I wanted to examine more closely. If these entrepreneurs had moved so quickly to build brands, what exactly had caused that change in such a short period of time? What changes in the labor force are forcing Chinese companies to go upstream? Was it due to soaring real estate prices, commodity markets, or something else? Visits to Chinese factories answered my questions.

CASE STUDIES
WHAT TO DO AND WHAT NOT TO DO IN CHINA

- Do Not Underestimate Domestic Chinese Brands' Quality

Western executives often foolishly scoff that Chinese brands could never compete with Western ones on anything but price. "They do not have the branding ability or focus on quality like the Japanese have," one global executive told me. He is underestimating the competition—never a smart thing to do.

Not only has the day arrived when many Chinese firms offer products that are as good as Western goods, but many compete head to head on quality and innovation. The Chinese business landscape is littered with global number one brands that failed when they hit China's shores. Critics complain that the government creates an uneven playing field by supporting domestic firms over foreign ones, but the reality is that search engine firm Google lost to Baidu because Baidu's technology for Chinese-language search was far better. Internet auction site eBay lost to Taobao because Taobao adopted an escrow-like pay system called Alipay that limited fraud, while eBay used PayPal.

Among the Chinese product companies starting to compete against Western brands is telecom giant Huawei, poised to overtake Ericsson as the world's largest network equipment maker, was recently chosen by Tele2 and Telenor over Ericsson in Sweden to install a 4G telecommunications system. Construction manufacturer LiuGong sells similar products to Caterpillar and Terex for 20 percent less. In interviews with dealers and end customers that my firm conducted, the majority said that for most projects, Chinese brands were more than good enough. China's wealthiest person in 2011 was the founder of construction giant SANY, Liang Wengen, who is worth over $9 billion.

Chinese companies are often able to cut operating costs and set prices below those of foreign brands while still offering comparable quality. To combat rising Chinese brands, Western brands might need to launch secondary brands, acquire Chinese ones, or shape the market to ensure premium positioning.

Key Action Item

Foreign brands should not discount the rise of Chinese brands. They are aggressive and well capitalized, and are spending increasing amounts of money on research and development. They are recruiting armies of engineering graduates from top universities around the world to bolster R&D. To compete, foreign brands must continue to innovate to maintain a technological advantage, cut costs by tightening production processes, or launch or acquire secondary brands to compete directly.

- Chinese Love Chinese Brands, Too

  Overall, Chinese trust foreign brands more than domestic ones not to cut corners in the production process. This is especially true in the luxury sector, where foreign brands are viewed as having more refinement and appealing brand heritages.

  Don't think Chinese brands will never beat foreign ones on anything but price, however. Given the choice, Chinese consumers tend to prefer local brands if they feel they are as good as the foreign competition. Buying Chinese brands appeals to rising nationalism, and Chinese believe domestic brands can better capture local flavors and scents.

  Mengniu Dairy and Haier are examples of companies that even wealthy Chinese consumers will often choose over foreign brands like Danone and Siemens. Mengniu charges more for their high-end yogurt products than Danone and most other foreign brands to emphasize high-quality ingredients. They use flavors that cater specifically to Chinese. When I interviewed dairy-section heads of supermarket chains, the majority told me that wealthy consumers prefer high-end domestic brands over foreign brands made in China, because they think a truly good Chinese brand will have better quality control than a foreign one.

Likewise, many wealthy Chinese prefer to buy Haier air conditioners and refrigerators, instead of German, Japanese, and Korean brands like Siemens and Samsung, out of nationalism and the perception that premium Chinese brands are globally best in class.

Key Action Item

Western brands should not assume Chinese will always prefer foreign brands over domestic ones, and that consumers always view foreign brands as more premium. Chinese will often prefer domestic brands, like Haier's consumer appliances, over foreign ones if they feel they are world-class brands. When competing in select consumer-market product categories, as Danone Yogurt is doing versus Mengniu, foreign brands might need to position themselves as cheaper alternatives if a domestic Chinese brand is viewed as having a premium position.

- Chinese Are Often Short Sighted Because Rules Can Change Quickly

  It is often very difficult for Chinese businesses to plan long term—not because executives are short sighted, but because rules and regulations change so quickly. For instance, many street-level Chinese stores are ramshackle and do not have nice fittings. The reason? Shop owners do not want to waste money because they fear real estate redevelopment will force them to move. Brands that create a comfortable ambiance move to high-priced malls or recently developed zones. Once urban planning gets more settled, Chinese brands will spend more on nicer shopping environments. In the meantime, smart ones save their money.

  For instance, right now most Chinese buyers of luxury products like to do their shopping abroad. Recent initiatives to make

Hainan Island a duty-free zone and to reduce tariffs on imported goods could change the luxury retail landscape overnight.

Key Action Item

Company executives need to keep abreast of potential new regulations that could severely impact their businesses. If they do not, they could suddenly find that they have invested in the wrong sectors and locations.

- Real Estate Is Intentionally Ramshackle

    Many Westerners say Chinese real estate companies exhibit poor urban planning. A common complaint by visiting Westerners is that malls are not built attractively, or that parking lots are constructed in prime building locations, like on a riverside, while shopping complexes and restaurant zones are built across the street without good river views. Criticism like this does not survive basic analysis. Rules force developers to start construction soon after buying land from the government. It is illegal to hold on to land as an investment, so real estate developers who think that land values will continue to rise either will build something as cheaply as possible, in the hopes of knocking everything down and rebuilding when prices go up, or will put up parking lots to fulfill regulatory requirements and delay prime construction on the property until later.

Key Action Item

Simply writing off or underestimating Chinese executives' long-term strategic thinking because they seem to be building inefficient projects is unwise, because they often have good reasons for holding off on investing and for trying to make money in the short term.

2

CHEAP CHINESE LABOR? NOT ANYMORE

CHINA'S WORKERS ARE DEMANDING BETTER PAY AND BETTER CONDITIONS— AND THEY ARE EARNING THEM

I opened my car door and was punched with jabs of heat that made me feel like I was stepping into a furnace. A thick layer of brackish grime immediately coated the car's hood. No matter how often I cleaned it, grit from the filth that blankets the whole country—created by endless construction and peasants burning garbage—seemed to swaddle the vehicle instantly.

To my left I saw a balding security guard in a golf cart, signaling me to follow him toward the entrance to what seemed like the world's largest building. I was about as far as possible from the gilded meeting room at the Okura Garden Hotel. Instead of billionaires and millionaires, I was about to meet the backbone of Chinese society: thousands of factory workers, whose sacrifices while toiling far from home had helped the country gain much-needed foreign hard currency in the 1990s by making products for Americans.

I was visiting the two-million-square-foot Shanghai factory of Laura Furniture, one of the world's largest furniture manufacturers. Many of the sofas Americans buy come from this factory, or one of its sister facilities down in Guangzhou in southern China. I was there to discuss with Bob, the president of the company, how to deal with rising labor costs and an appreciating renminbi.

The combination of the two was killing Laura Furniture's margins, Bob had told me on a crackling Skype call the previous week, and he was looking for strategies to adapt to the changing trends. He needed me to come to see their operations and help them figure out what to do.

Bob told me Laura had faced the same problems in America two decades earlier, when rising labor costs and improved global shipping convinced them to shut their factories in the Midwest and relocate to China in search of a limitless supply of cheap labor. The problem was that cheap Chinese labor had started to disappear in recent years, as Chinese workers demanded better pay. In search of even cheaper labor, Laura Furniture had already opened up large plants in Vietnam and Indonesia several years earlier. But they found the workers there less productive and the transportation infrastructure weak, Bob said, forcing them to consider other strategies.

I met Bob at the entrance to the factory. His meaty hand reached out and shook mine vigorously with a hard grip. Bob was in his mid-fifties and looked like he was dressed head to foot in Dockers. He looked fit; probably a former high school football star, I thought, though the creep of middle age and perhaps too many large, American portions of hamburgers and French fries were starting to show on his belly. As Bob and I started to walk the factory floor, I quickly realized I would not need to do my cardio exercises that night. It would take us 30 minutes to walk at a good clip from one end of the floor to the other.

There were over 10,000 workers on the factory floor. Row after row of women bent over long counters, sewing cushions and pillows. Men were nailing armrests and stapling faux wood to make chairs and bookcases to deck out the middle American homes, the kind with gnomes on the lawn and collectibles over fake fireplaces.

The factory was worlds apart from the sweatshop image many Americans have of Chinese factories, and 180 degrees different from the factories I visited when I first arrived in China over a decade earlier. There were no disgusting fumes swamping the work area or unsecured pipes dangling from the ceilings; no slave-driving managers swaggering around, prodding workers to move faster; no chains and bars locking the windows and doors.

Laura's factory looked more like a giant, modern sports stadium or one of the dazzling airports opening up all over the country. In contrast to the outdoors, where my car was steadily accumulating an extra coating or two of dirt, the work areas were clean and brightly lit. The air was fine to breathe, and didn't make me cough or cause my throat burn. Workers varnishing wood pieces wore facemasks and were in well-fumigated areas away from the tailors. While the workers were largely silent, it was not because they were afraid to talk; rather, they were intent on doing their jobs and hitting performance targets to get bonuses.

Bob is a real salt-of-the-earth guy. He looks at you straight in the eye when talking. You could easily picture him as the head coach of your child's Little League baseball team, or maybe as president of your local Kiwanis Club.

As I made my way across the factory floor, still dazzled by the sheer size of the place, Bob pointed out the red safety lights at the top of each workstation. If a problem occurred on the production line, he said, a worker would hit a switch to flick on the red light, and one of the supervisors, clad in an orange smock, would come right over. Production in that work area would stop until the potential hazard was fixed satisfactorily.

Line workers and supervisors were paid not just by how much they produced, Bob told me, but also for the prevention of workplace accidents. Not only was this the right thing to do, he said, but it also met increasing worker and government demand for safer work environments via more-expensive technology and best-practice management methods. It was important for Laura that workers in China felt like they were part of the Laura family, so they brought the same codes of conduct (no swearing, for instance) and regulations from their American operations to China.

Other companies across China were also installing top-notch production lines in their factories, much as Laura had done. In 2008, Aircraft maker Airbus opened a giant plant in Tianjin, its most state-of-the-art factory and its first final-assembly line outside of Europe. Luxury auto firm Mercedes-Benz announced in 2011 that it would invest a further 30 billion renminbi (almost $5 billion) to produce more cars for sale in China, because it could no longer keep up with demand through imports alone.

New factories being erected across the country resulted in an employee's labor market, because the factories being built needed a dependable workforce. They were offering huge salary increases and bonuses. Bob told me his biggest nightmare was recruiting and retaining talent. Unlike a decade before, when workers seemed to beg for jobs, and lines of them huddled at the factory gates looking for work, he now faced too many disruptions in production because he could not find enough skilled workers. Higher costs were becoming a serious issue, because salaries were going up as Laura had to fend off poaching from other factories nearby. Bob estimated that total labor costs might double by 2015; no longer were they a small part of the operating expense of running a factory in China.

Perhaps counterintuitively, the labor pool actually dried up during the great financial crisis, as Americans and Europeans increased investment in China to offset flagging sales in their home markets. The tight labor pool was evident not just at the low end in factories, but also in the white-collar labor force. Technology companies such as Microsoft, Intel, and Google—even after it stopped offering its search engine in China—have embarked on huge hiring sprees or have set up research and development centers there. Citigroup announced it would triple its head count on the mainland within three years to 10,000, not for back-office needs but to cater to local clients. Pepsi, Coca-Cola, and Disney all have announced multibillion-dollar investments. Investment banks like Goldman Sachs are increasing their business in China even as they pare their ranks in New York and London.

The result is massive competition among employers to hire workers in China—even at the height of the financial crisis, when billionaire investor Warren Buffett declared that America's economy had fallen off a cliff. It has become so easy for workers to find jobs elsewhere that they job-hop constantly. Desperate for warm bodies, companies are throwing 20 percent or greater salary increases at workers to steal them from other firms, creating huge paydays for executive recruiters and headaches for general managers.

Bob's human resource problems are mirrored in company after company. My firm conducted interviews in 2010 with human resource managers and senior executives at Fortune 500 companies. More than 70 percent of respondents said they had annual employee turnover of 30 percent or higher. Nearly 90 percent of the companies reported that their biggest obstacle to growth in the coming five years was not the topics the Western media reports about all the time—corruption, copyright infringement, and rising protectionism—but the ability to recruit and retain talent. In comparison, an 11 percent turnover rate in America is considered way too high and detrimental to business.

One Italian general manager of a small production facility making furnishings and accessories for retail stores told me over lunch that 50 percent of his factory workers leave within two months, no matter how much training and pay he offered them. There was always some factory owner who would offer a little more, even for unqualified workers, because demand for warm bodies was so high. The lack of trained workers was hurting his ability to hit growth targets and meet client demand for products. He was so frustrated, he could not sleep at night and was smoking more.

A New Zealand factory owner, who had facilities in southern China that produced electronic road signs, told me he took 10 employees to Dubai as part of a retention strategy. It failed, he said, because in job negotiations with other firms, they all touted that they had been to Dubai to demonstrate that they were worldly, globe-trotting executives. Within three months of the Dubai trip, three of the employees had left. He was shutting many of his factories in China, and looking to markets like

Mongolia, where employee turnover was less of a problem and costs were stable.

As I made my way to the Laura Furniture factory dining room, Bob outlined more of the problems his company was facing. Aside from labor costs going up, he explained, the declining U.S. dollar was further eroding margins and hitting his business hard. Because Laura's factories are all overseas, a declining dollar means his input costs for production in China or Vietnam are going up, while the end price to American consumers is staying the same, or even dropping as he has to discount more to get Americans to open their wallets. Homeowners were putting off buying new furniture, and in all his decades doing business he had never seen American consumer confidence so low.

It is an understatement to say he was angry at the calls of U.S. government officials (like New York Senator Chuck Schumer) for China to let its currency appreciate, or that he was frustrated with Federal Reserve chief Ben Bernanke's decision to increase the money supply through quantitative easing. These wrong headed policies, he said, just caused more investors to flee the greenback and switch their investment portfolios to commodities or foreign markets, where there were greater possibilities to receive higher returns, and which further increased Bob's input prices. He did not see commodity prices stabilizing in the near future until the greenback regained its strength and the debt situation in the eurozone stabilized.

Breaking it down further, Bob showed how an appreciating renminbi cut into his company's profits. If salaries, rents, and commodity prices went up at a conservative 10 percent a year, and the renminbi appreciated 5 percent annually, that meant his overall costs would rise 15 percent a year. Rising costs would not be a big problem if he could raise prices in America, but he worried about doing so, with American

unemployment still hovering close to 10 percent and consumer confidence at decade lows.

For Bob, the combination of the depreciating dollar and rising costs in China is eroding margins, which means lowering
bonuses, salaries, and dividends for American senior management. He told me the problem he was facing was also happen-
ing to most of his peers in the American business community
who had already shifted production to China.

Once I got Bob going about the state of the global economy, he couldn't stop. An appreciating renminbi wouldn't save
American jobs either, as economist Paul Krugman had been saying it would on the *New York Times* op-ed page. "That 'saving
American jobs' argument is ridiculous," Bob said. "How many
firms realistically will go back to America? They're going to look
for even cheaper production locales. Krugman doesn't understand business, just theory." As labor costs rose, Laura Furniture
had opened factories in cheaper countries like Vietnam and
Indonesia, but certainly not America.

Relocating to Vietnam and leaving China completely is not a
solution, Bob admitted, frustration creeping into his voice. He
said Chinese workers overall have more experienced line managers, and more drive and ability to produce more sophisticated
products. "Our Chinese workers produce more pieces with far
superior quality, given the same amount of time, than our workers in Vietnam," he said. "In China, it seems like they know if
they do well, they can get promoted and make a lot of money
in the future. In Vietnam and Indonesia, the workers do not
seem to see that they can go up and make a lot of money eventually, so they move at a more measured pace."

Equally important, the level of infrastructure development in
Vietnam and Indonesia was 30 years behind China's. "Vietnam
just doesn't have the roads and shipping facilities that China has,"

Bob said. He told me Vietnam and Indonesia are efficient markets for relatively simple manufacturing, like apparel or athletic shoes, but not for more complicated or time-sensitive pieces like bedroom sets or the latest electronic gadgets. As a result, Bob was forced to keep all of his higher-end production in China, despite the rising costs, and was planning to raise end prices to American consumers as soon as he could or else take reduced margins. He was now using his factories in Vietnam and Indonesia to reduce costs at the lower end of the production scale.

The shortage of skilled Chinese laborers and subsequent rising costs made me wonder exactly how much the factory workers in China were making now. A senior Chinese seamstress—typically a 22-year-old with four or five years' experience—earned about $800 a month—three or four times the wages in Vietnam, Bob told me. That is an astounding number, I thought. I recalled from an internal study a colleague of mine had done to benchmark my firm's starting salaries that entry-level, university-educated workers at white-collar firms like Deloitte and Citigroup made similar wages. I wondered how young Chinese auditors and investment bank analysts and their parents felt when they found out that factory workers sewing cushions or stapling headboards were making more than they were. A university degree was supposed to be their ticket to riches.

Bob also highlighted a trend that I, too, had started seeing when interviewing Chinese families around the country. Women were starting to outearn men, changing family dynamics and the role of women in society. In Bob's factories, women tended to make more than men because they could do the higher-skilled sewing of sofa covers, which took significant training, while men tended to do more heavy labor that required little training. Women also seemed more intent on working hard and beating manager expectations, Bob said.

When I asked Bob why he and other business leaders were not more publicly stating their case against Congress for their calls to let the renminbi appreciate, Bob said that the anti-China rhetoric and general frustration was so serious in America right now that he feared backlash from Congress or everyday Americans. It was better to keep his head down, he said, and lobby privately rather than publicly, in case someone decided to make an example of Laura and demonize them—even though China's rise meant more job creation for Americans working for Laura.

Bob's human resource situation brought home the clear, countrywide labor trends that are heralding the End of Cheap China. Chinese workers, no longer desperate for any job that will put food on the table, will not settle for low monthly wages or horrible working conditions. Compared to just a decade ago, there are now too many job opportunities available to them, and they are too confident about the country's future. The government has also been pushing up minimum wages to better protect employee rights, and to promote a shift away from manufacturing to a consumption- and services-oriented economy. In 2011, 21 of China's 31 provinces raised the minimum wage by an average of 21.7 percent; in 2010, Sichuan Province alone raised it by 44 percent. Cheap Chinese workers, one could say, are becoming as scarce as cheap, sexy prostitutes.

Relocating manufacturing operations out of China completely, however, is not really an alternative for many companies, since China's skilled workers are more numerous and better than those in other countries, and it has an unrivaled, world-class infrastructure, as Laura's experiences in Vietnam and Indonesia have shown. The result is soaring costs, which will erode margins for American companies unless they transfer higher prices to U.S. consumers, or enter new consumer markets to offset weakening U.S. and European consumer demand.

Ultimately, Bob and I developed the solution to convert half of Laura's Shanghai factory to produce furniture to sell within China. After all, retail sales there have been growing 16 to 18 percent a year for the last five years, as incomes rise and millions of Chinese buy their first homes and move into livable housing for the first time.

By selling into China, rather than looking at it solely as a manufacturing base for export, Bob could not only tap into the wallets of China's rising middle class, but he could price his furniture in renminbi. Even if the currency continued to appreciate as the central government indicated it would, he would not have to worry about raising prices in foreign currency fluctuations. The other half of his factory would continue to produce for export from China, but Bob knew his real growth opportunities were going to come from selling to the domestic Chinese consumer. The market was evolving so rapidly that no furniture player had been able to consolidate market share across the whole country, which was his goal. Successfully penetrating the Chinese market would not only save jobs back in America for Laura, but also create new ones.

Bob's story at Laura Furniture is far from rare. Over the past three years, as America muddles through a jobless economic recovery, more and more brands have been converting their factories in China from producing mostly export goods to making products to sell within China.

Jacob, the Asia-Pacific marketing head of an international office products firm, told me, "It is just not viable anymore to produce cheaply in China, but it is also impossible in the short-term to replace China as a main manufacturing hub. Other countries simply do not have the infrastructure, skilled workers, and mid-management needed to replace China completely." He told me he had decided to keep all of his manufacturing facilities in China, but was converting his sales forces to try to sell within China. He was hiring new employees to oversee development within China and signing deals with sales-channel partners all over the country. So far, his initiatives had become profitable. As Jacob left my office, he said, "It will take other countries another generation at least before they can truly rival China in manufacturing prowess. They just don't have the work-force or infrastructure to compete."

Labor pool changes are disrupting China's manufacturing sector and forcing business models to evolve. Newer firms, like the ones run by the entrepreneurs I met at the Okura Garden Hotel, are building new brands that can charge a premium for their products and services and be sold to consumers who are not price sensitive. Other firms like Laura Furniture are able to adapt by converting factories to sell within China. Yet thousands of smaller Chinese factories, including many furniture makers, have closed down in the last three years due to paper-thin margins and an inability to tap credit lines. The industry is consolidating; smaller producers are unable to make money as the appreciating renminbi decimates their margins, and profits become dependent upon volume and production efficiency rather than low price.

Massive, efficient players like Foxconn, the Taiwanese electronics manufacturing behemoth that makes many of Apple and Dell's products, are leveraging economies of scale to shore up market share and grab even more. The scope of some of their operations is hard to imagine.

In the last two years, Foxconn has relocated 350,000 of its factory workers from Shenzhen in southern China to a massive new factory in Henan Province, in the central part of the country. This move is comparable to moving the entire population of New Orleans (343,829 in the 2010 U.S. Census) to New Mexico.

They have more employees than the entire population of Iceland (319,062, according to a 2009 World Bank estimate).

Foxconn has been rumored to be investing billions of dollars in setting up factories in South America to find cheaper options, but it has relocated its manufacturing in China to other places in country rather than shifting out completely. To combat rising labor costs, it announced plans in 2011 to install one million robots in its Chinese factories to replace workers over the next several years.

They are more like midsized American cities than factories, and they dwarf Laura Furniture's facility. In addition to factories, companies such as Foxconn have to establish local dormitories, hospitals, and leisure areas.

Foxconn was compelled to improve conditions and raise salaries after a public firestorm in 2010 surrounding 18 attempted worker suicides at its Shenzhen factory, which resulted in 14 deaths. Foxconn faced heavy criticism, not just from international groups but also from Chinese media, academics, and ordinary people who commented on online forums about harsh working conditions. Foxconn responded by increasing worker salaries by 66 percent in the months following the controversy. Around the same time, Honda raised salaries at its plant in Guangdong Province by 32 percent after workers began striking.

The companies with the best-designed and best-operated compounds, and the most comfortable living conditions for their employees, will be the winners in attracting and retaining talent as the labor pool continues to tighten. This also creates a more expensive labor-cost landscape that boxes out factories unable to afford higher costs.

America's economic growth for the past three decades can be largely attributed to the willingness of Chinese laborers to slave away, underpaid, in factories that make the products Americans love—Apple computers, Nike shoes, and Gap khakis. Low wages have generated massive profits for U.S. firms that chose to relocate to or source from factories in China, like Walmart, and have made consumer electronics and clothes affordable for everyday Americans. This process fueled America's addiction to consumption while keeping inflation low, despite loose U.S. monetary policies and an unhealthy addiction to debt that traces back to the Reagan years.

For decades, this arrangement was seen as win-win for all involved, when the American business community and free-trade economists prevailed in their argument to reduce tariffs to promote outsourcing. Middle-class Americans filled their homes with product after product for stunningly low prices, while Chinese workers earned enough to eat and have basic shelter over their heads. But this arrangement started to unravel during the financial crisis.

As more Americans lost their jobs, China came to be viewed as a scapegoat for U.S. unemployment, rather than for the real reasons: poor regulation of Wall Street; a bickering political system; and average Americans' addiction to debt, which went on for far too long. Now one hears the constant refrain from politicians and commentators on TV that China is stealing U.S. manufacturing jobs and that Americans should only buy products made in America. For these talking heads, China's rise is a zero-sum game with the United States.

While such arguments appeal to patriotic pride, giving in to these sentiments hurts Americans more than it helps them. Without China, many American families would not be able to afford quality furniture or the latest technology. If businesses like Laura or Apple were forced to bring their factories back to America, their prices would rise tenfold, causing rampant inflation and further hurting consumer sentiment and it is even doubtful these jobs would build consumer confidence if they came back. Few Americans are willing to work for low wages in factories, as their forefathers did in the textile and footwear mills of New England.

Even at the height of the financial crisis with 24 million Americans unemployed, with Occupy Wall Street protests erupting across America, thousands of farm jobs in America have gone unfilled, because so many Americans don't want to work in those conditions. However, the Obama administration has deported a record high of nearly one million illegal immigrants—the very people who were willing to take those jobs. Aside from plentiful jobs causing Chinese wages to rise, there are simply fewer workers, because the one-child policy implemented in 1978 has resulted in an aging population today. The magazine *Science* found that 22.9 percent of the Chinese population was under the age of 14 in 2000. That number dropped to only 16.6 percent in 2010. Unless the government eases population control laws soon, or allows workers from neighboring countries like Myanmar and Vietnam to work in China, it is doubtful that the labor pool will grow anytime soon.

Economists like Cai Fang of the Chinese Academy of Social Sciences, and Ross Garnaut of the Australian National University, have suggested that China has reached the Lewisian turning point, named for the Saint Lucian developmental economist Arthur Lewis, who won the Nobel Prize for Economics in 1979. Lewis claimed that once the supply of surplus labor in developing countries diminishes, industrial wages begin to rise quickly.

Fewer and fewer Chinese employees are willing to work in factories, as they too want to enjoy an American-style lifestyle of consumption, and seek more comfortable jobs closer to their families. Changes to the Chinese labor pool are, for the most part, healthy for the economy and a sign of growth. Better-paying jobs and more efficient factories will help reduce the all-encompassing pollution that seems to plague the country, and will help China overcome the mid-income gap many countries hit when the average per capita GDP hits $6,000. For China to avoid ending up economically like Mexico, where income gaps between the rich and poor are getting wider, it must continue to push for higher-paying jobs and a greater dispersion of wealth.

All these changes have created a confident labor pool that is forcing companies to deal with rising labor and real estate costs. Some companies cope with the End of Cheap China by building brands and charging more for their products, as the billionaires at the Okura Garden Hotel have done; others by consolidating market share and becoming a volume player, such as Foxconn; and still others by converting factories to sell within China and other emerging markets. It is doubtful that rising costs will send manufacturing jobs back to the United States. What is more likely is that China's economic rise will create more job opportunities and profits for American companies that can evolve with the new status quo instead of holding onto the past. History is littered with examples of companies and countries that were unable to adjust to new conditions.

As I looked around at the workers in front of me at Laura's factory, I wondered what, aside from a shrinking labor pool and more job opportunities, had made all these workers seem so optimistic. Nearly every Chinese person I have met brims with confidence and an expectation that life will get better for them and their children. They are not blind. They see problems like corruption or pollution in society every day, but overall they perceive their lives getting measurably better, and expect them to continue to do so.

This confidence did not come into being overnight, or just because salaries increased in the last few years. Their optimism and satisfaction with life are the culmination of 30 years of opportunities and political reforms, which have created a freer and healthier society than China has ever seen. In order to see why China's labor pool is so confident, why the economy is growing so well, and why the government implements the laws it does, it is important to look at China's recent past.

CASE STUDIES

WHAT TO DO AND WHAT NOT TO DO IN CHINA

- Rethink the Location of Manufacturing Operations

    Salaries for blue-collar workers are soaring by double-digit percentages due to government pressure for better employment protections, worker demands, and a shrinking labor pool. To offset rocketing labor costs, companies need to rethink manufacturing and sourcing strategies. Light-industry companies especially might need to relocate operations to countries like Vietnam and Indonesia. Nike now produces more of its products in Vietnam than in China (37 vs. 34 percent).

    China's infrastructure is far superior to other Asian countries, and worker efficiency is higher as well, which means companies higher up the value chain should think about moving to the central part of China or automating production lines before quitting the country altogether. Foxconn, the maker of many Apple products like the iPhone and iPad, as well as Dell products, relocated 350,000 workers to central China and has announced plans to add one million robots to their factories to replace workers. Intel has built large chip facilities in Chengdu and Dalian, and has shifted jobs there from Shanghai.

Key Action Item

Companies will have to deal with long-term trends of rising labor wages and a shrinking labor pool by moving inland in China or to lower-cost countries, automating production lines, or building more premium brands that have fatter margins.

- View China as a Market to Sell Into, Not Just to Produce In

    Apple no longer views China only as a production base, but as a key market. Retail sales in China are growing 16 to 18 percent a year. Consumer spending is poised to continue, as the government promotes consumption to wean the country away from relying too much on high-polluting exports. Consumption accounts for 42 percent of the economy, up from a third a decade ago, and CMR predicts it will account for 50 percent within five years.

    After a slow start in opening official Apple stores, Apple's sales in China quadrupled from $3 billion in 2010 to $12 billion in 2011—despite the fact that iPhones and iPads are 30 percent more expensive than in the United States. Apple initially made the mistake of waiting too long to roll out new products in China. It delayed the release of new versions of the iPhone more than a year after the U.S. launch, which caused Chinese consumers to buy Apple products smuggled in from Hong Kong or the United States on the gray market, rather than through licensed Apple resellers. Analysts estimate two and a half million iPhones have unofficially been sold in China. Apple turned its retail operations around by introducing new products like the iPad in China soon after their release in America, obviating the need for anxious consumers to buy in the gray market. Chinese consumers are well aware of what products you are selling in other markets, because of information flow via the Internet and tourism, and they don't want to wait months or years to buy the newest products. They have no compunctions about going through illegal channels if it means faster gratification.

Key Action Item

Your former factory workers now might be your target market. With rising incomes, per capita GDP has tripled in the last decade from $1,000 to $3,000 per year. Revamp your China-based factories to sell within China rather than just for export.

- Release in China before Other Markets

    Many companies make the mistake of taking too long to introduce the season's newest products into China. Until Apple moved up its scheduled release dates for China, their official sales stumbled because consumers were not willing to wait a month before getting access to their devices. Over 50 million Chinese traveled abroad in 2010 to countries where they can buy the latest products. Even consumers who do not travel check these items out, discuss them in Internet chat rooms, and get angry and frustrated if brands delay their release in China.

    Instead, companies should think about launching in China first, or at least as soon as they launch in other markets. Porsche launched its Panamera sedan in China before doing so in the United States. China is now Porsche's second-largest market globally, reporting in July 2011 that year-over-year sales grew 500 percent. Likewise, Ferrari often releases new cars in China before America.

Key Action Item

China can no longer be viewed as a secondary market. To sell inside China successfully, companies must reengineer supply chains to offer products there as early as possible after release. For premium products such as iPhones that tourists can buy abroad and fit easily into their luggage, companies should consider releasing in China first.

3

STABILITY IS THE KEY TO HAPPINESS

HOW CHINA'S GOVERNMENT THINKS AND WHY IT ACTS THE WAY IT DOES

The first time I met Lili Li one sweltering Beijing day in 2001, I was nervous. She was no longer the movie star and sex symbol who ruled the Chinese box office along with Ruan Lingyu and Butterfly Wu in the 1930s and 1940s, but an elderly woman in her eighties, decades past her time in the limelight. I was nervous not because I had taught about her films when I was instructing undergraduates as a Harvard Teaching Fellow, but because she was about to become my grandmother-in-law, and I wanted to make a good first impression.

The Beijing traffic was terrible that day, as it is most days, and my fiancée Jessica and I were two hours late to our meeting. Not a way to make a good first impression, I thought. Neither were the streaks of sludge on the bottom of my khakis that must have wiped off from the car door as I got out.

I entered a sparsely decorated home and was led to the living room, where Lili Li waited for us. The only indications that we were in the home of a movie star were the dozens of oil paintings by famed painter Ai Zhongxin, Lili Li's second husband, lining the walls. A copy of Ai's famous revolutionary piece, depicting the torment of China's countryside in the pre-Communist era, hung next to one detailing the tribulations of the Long March. My favorite was of a young Lili Li in her heyday as a movie actress, with her famous large, doe-like eyes and long, flowing, jet-black hair.

Sitting on a wooden chair drinking tea as I entered the room was Lili Li. Her hair had turned a grayish white, and she wore a simple floral shirt. As I walked over to sit next to her, she met me with a warm smile and a hug. Although she was no longer movie-star beautiful, she still had that star quality that lights up a room.

Within minutes, Lili Li had taken me by surprise. Rather than talk pleasantries, as I had expected, she immediately started to tell me about the pain of the Cultural Revolution (1966–1976) and her searing hatred for Jiang Qing, known to the Western world as Madame Mao, leader of the dreaded Gang of Four. Lili Li welcomed me into the family by teaching me about what it had suffered for standing against tyranny.

The pain of the Cultural Revolution was not easily forgotten for Lili Li. Until that day, I had mostly read about the Cultural Revolution in textbooks, heard about it from Western professors, or seen snippets of the turmoil in Western movies, but Lili Li brought the pain and horror to life.

She began by telling me about Luo Jingyu, her first husband, a famed filmmaker and head of the China Film Studio, who had received an award from President Franklin D. Roosevelt for resisting Japanese aggression during World War II. During the Cultural Revolution, Red Guards, the radical and violent student groups, hounded her husband as they did many elites. Wielding the Red Guards as an instrument of terror, the Gang of Four sought personal power under the cloak of advancing socialism and class struggle. Elites throughout the country were tortured, jailed, or murdered during the tumult. Universities were shut down for a decade, and the country lost decades of progress.

Red Guards tortured Lili Li's husband until he could bear the pain no more and committed suicide. His body was never found. Only his eyeglasses were returned to her.

Lili Li had also suffered personal torture and public humiliation. Red Guards shaved her hair in front of a seething mob, and hung posters denouncing her in large characters around the country's capital. They harassed her whole family. Due to malnourishment and stress, my mother-in-law gave birth to my wife and her identical twin sister several months early. My wife remains beautiful but petite, a subtle reminder of China's dark past and its ongoing ramifications.

Hearing Lili Li speak of the horror of the Cultural Revolution, I kept asking myself: What could she have done to warrant such suffering? Why was she singled out? How many others suffered because of evil politicians? Lili Li's story, as it turns out, sheds light on the Gang of Four; it explains the harsh past of many of China's current leaders, how it makes them act the way they do, and why so many Chinese are optimistic about their futures.

The story starts 80 years earlier, when Bette Davis and Betty Grable ruled Hollywood's silver screen and Yankee greats Lou Gehrig and Joe DiMaggio dominated the baseball diamond. Lili

Li was China's marquee actress and led a Hollywood lifestyle, counting international megastars like Charlie Chaplin as close friends.

At that time, a C-list actress called Lan Ping entered Lili Li's sphere. She appeared in several movies alongside Lili Li in lesser parts. Lan Ping was good-looking enough to make it into movies, but not memorable enough to capture the hearts of audiences. Known for her fiery temper, Lan Ping battled everyone around her, directors and fellow stars alike, jockeying for better parts and more money. She rarely got her way. Perhaps it was because she lacked talent, or maybe it was just because audiences could sense ice in her heart, but she never became famous until decades later.

Driven by clawing ambition and a willingness to step on others, Lan Ping scored her largest role as the fourth wife of Mao Zedong and the cornerstone of the Gang of Four. She changed her name to Jiang Qing, and began using violence to gain power and exact personal vendettas.

Jiang Qing hated Lili Li and her family personally. She blamed Lili Li and her husband Luo for preventing her rise to stardom. She also hated Lili Li because she came from a heavyweight political background that could limit her power.

Lili Li's father, Qian Zhuangfei, was an early hero of the Chinese Communist Party, which he had joined in 1925. Unlike many of the early members, Qian came from a wealthy background and gave up a life of comfort to help the masses. He traced his lineage back to Zhang Tingyu, a powerful premier for several decades during the Qing Dynasty under Qing emperors Kangxi, Yongzheng, and Qianlong in the seventeenth and eighteenth centuries.

Qian also had been close friends with Prime Minister Zhou Enlai, whom Jiang Qing despised. Many predicted Qian would become the future prime minister because of his belief in Communism and broad-based support.

Qian became a double agent for the Communists during the bitter Chinese Civil War (1927–1949) between the Nationalists and Communists. Under Chiang Kai-shek's Nationalist Party, he was in charge of rooting out Communists. Few thought someone with such a gilded background as Qian would turn to his back on riches to become Communist and help the masses.

After ruthlessly torturing a Communist Party member, Chiang Kai-shek discovered Mao Zedong and Zhou Enlai's hiding place. In order to warn the two prominent Communist leaders that they were about to be caught, Qian had to blow his cover. He became a personal target of Chiang Kai-shek and a hero of the Communist cause. Qian died during the Long March, a decisive but tortuous 8,000-mile trek the Communists undertook while being pursued and attacked by the Nationalists, before regrouping at Yan'an in Shaanxi province.

The Party proclaimed Qian a martyr for his sacrifice on the people's behalf. Monuments have been erected around the country, and schoolchildren still learn about his exploits and sacrifice for the masses. The Chinese Communist Party recently named Qian one of the 50 most important party members in history, despite having been killed over a decade before the official founding of the People's Republic of China in 1949. Out of friendship and gratitude to Qian for saving his life, Zhou Enlai went out of his way to care for Qian's daughter, Lili Li.

During the Cultural Revolution, Jiang Qing sought to eradicate threats to her dominance and exact revenge for petty offenses. She attacked Lili Li's family with a vengeance reserved for her most bitter enemies and rivals. As Lili Li continued to relate the pain her family had endured to create a better life for everyday Chinese, her eyes turned sad.

In the years before she passed away in 2005, Lili Li continued to tell me more about the evil that Jiang Qing perpetrated, and how it is the duty of a people blessed with so much to do what is right—even in the face of tyranny. She reinforced the importance of standing up to evil and sacrificing for the country. She had even told my wife, Jessica, when she went to America for graduate studies in finance at Boston College, that it was her duty to return to China to help reform the financial system and help make it strong. A life that did not help the country wasted all the sacrifices of previous generations.

What most surprised me about our conversations was when Lili Li told me that, overall, she liked Mao Zedong. She mostly blamed Jiang Qing and the Gang of Four for the tyranny and suffering they had caused the nation. Sure, Mao made mistakes, she said, especially as he aged, but overall he did good things for China.

For me, whose view of Mao until then had been mostly shaped by Western professors and media, I was surprised that she had anything nice to say about the former supreme leader. Westerners portrayed him as evil, on par with Hitler or Stalin, who killed his own people to maintain power. I thought anyone who liked Mao likewise must have been evil, or brainwashed by Chinese propaganda. But Lili Li was not easily swayed by propaganda, cowed by fear, or complicit with the horrors of the Gang of Four. She was someone who personally knew Mao and other leaders, and who had suffered terribly during the Cultural Revolution for standing up to tyranny.

Listening to Lili Li, I began to question my preconceptions about China's government. If Lili Li, a hero for fighting tyranny and her sacrifice for the country, felt Mao Zedong was not pure evil and had actually done good for the people, what else could the Western media and academia have gotten wrong about China's leaders and the country overall?

As I spent more time meeting senior officials over the years in informal gatherings, my understanding of the leadership and how they acted started to change. I found the horrors of the Cultural Revolution were fresh and raw wounds for them, not a long-forgotten stage in history. Many Chinese look at contemporary problems through the lens of the suffering they experienced firsthand.

Being from America, where free speech is bedrock, censorship to me was the hallmark of a brutish yet frightened bureaucracy keeping a viselike grip on power. As I learned more, I realized my lens, having been directed by Western media, had analyzed China incorrectly.

Perhaps government actions that seem thuggish to Western observers are actually protective measures to ensure that the country never faces instability again, and that tyrants like Jiang Qing are prevented from rising. Chinese in general are happy because they compare their current lives with the past, and the progress is obvious to them. They look to freer societies like America as a different path; or perhaps the same one, but at a different stage of the journey.

Criticism of Chinese government actions by Western observers often stems from the misconception that the current leadership led the chaos of the Cultural Revolution. The opposite is most likely true, as many current leaders and their families suffered the most.

Lili Li's son Luo Dan, my father-in-law, eventually married the daughter of Marshal Ye Jianying, Ye Xiangzhen, sometimes known as Lingzi. Marshal Ye was ranked number three in the Party hierarchy during the Cultural Revolution, behind only Mao himself and Wang Hongwen one of the members of the

Gang of Four. Despite Marshal Ye's power, or perhaps because of it, his children were jailed during the Cultural Revolution, some in solitary confinement.

As soon as Mao died, Marshal Ye led the arrest of the Gang of Four. He acted as the president of the country in the 1980s when he was Chairman of the Standing Committee of the Politburo, China's highest governing body. Deng Xiaoping was another leader at the time; he ranked behind Marshal Ye in the Party chain of command and had also suffered at the hands of tyranny. His son, Deng Pufang, was paralyzed after the Red Guards threw him out of a three-story window at Peking University during the Cultural Revolution. Red Guards denied him medical treatment, which doctors later said might have saved his ability to walk, because his father had been denounced as a capitalist.

Together, Marshal Ye and Deng took charge of China and set the nation on its path towards reform, by creating stability and implementing broad-ranging market reforms that gave rise to today's economic growth. These two prominent political and military figures both suffered during the Cultural Revolution. As with Lili Li, this personal horror shaped their worldview and influenced their families. Ye's son, Ye Xuanping, who had also been jailed, became the governor of Guangdong and vice chairman of the People's Political Consultative Congress. One of Ye's daughters married Zou Jiahua, who became a vice premier. Another daughter married the former chairman of CITIC bank, the state-owned investment giant.

Xi Jinping, presumed to be China's next president, also suffered during the Cultural Revolution. He was sent to the countryside for a decade. His father, a former deputy prime minister, was removed from his position and jailed for 16 years. Tragedy also befell Bo Xilai, the current Party secretary of the western municipality of Chongqing and a rising star in the Party. His father, Bo Yibo, was one of the Party's Eight Immortals, a group of senior officials who held top positions of power in the 1980s and 1990s. Bo Yibo's entire family, including Bo Xilai, was jailed and shunted off to a labor camp for a decade. Yet Western analysts absurdly portray Bo Xilai as somehow wanting to return to the chaotic and violent days of the Cultural Revolution because of a "Red" patriotic campaign he is promoting in Chongqing.

Personal tragedy during the Cultural Revolution influences the worldview of China's leaders and citizens. Understanding China's recent history sheds light on people's day-to-day choices and optimism, and on government actions. Many Western analysts do not understand or underestimate the effects of recent history on contemporary society.

In his recent book *On China,* former U.S. Secretary of State Henry Kissinger analyzes Imperial China to provide a framework for understanding the nation and how America needs to deal with a returning superpower. Others try to use an outdated Confucian framework or a Sun Tzu–based military philosophy to explain the country today. Analyzing the Cultural Revolution, and the personal tragedies suffered during the tumult, is a more useful framework for understanding China's rise.

The issue of human rights and how to define them is a major point of contention in U.S.–China relations. Christian groups deem China's one-child policy evil. Supporters of the Dalai Lama and the World Uighur Congress argue that China suppresses their right of worship. In 2010, Google accused the government of trying to steal its code and stopped offering its search engine services in the Chinese market after it refused to censor itself. Critics denounced the government for blocking

access to social media websites like Facebook and Twitter after
the Muslim uprising in the northwestern region of Xinjiang,
which resulted in over 1,000 casualties, and after protests in Iran
were found to have been organized via social media. In a crackdown at the height of the Arab Spring, the government arrested
dissidents like the artist Ai Weiwei, who designed the Bird's Nest
Stadium for the 2008 Beijing Olympics, and kept Liu Xiaobo in
jail even as he became the 2010 Nobel Peace Prize winner.

Analysts like Elizabeth Economy from the Council on Foreign
Relations argue that the government is cracking down because
it fears being overthrown, like Mubarak in Egypt. In reality, it
is more likely that China's government is looking at decades of
strength. Discontent bubbles up at times, but Economy and
other analysts gloss over major differences between contemporary China and the conditions in the Middle East that gave rise
to the Arab Spring.

Unlike corrupt regimes in the Arab world, the Chinese government has diffused its power, so one family does not hold too
much. This has established a crucial system of checks and balances to prevent totalitarian leadership. Middle Eastern families,
like Mubarak's in Egypt or Zine al-Abidine Ben Ali's in Tunisia,
were able to rule for decades, but China has strict term limits
and retirement ages for even the most powerful officials.

Enforcing retirement ages and distribution of power has
allowed for peaceful transitions of power and competing interests within the Communist Party, even as it remains one party.
Most senior leaders do not come from the most powerful families; their offspring go into business to cement wealth, instead
of staying in government like the Mubaraks did to make money.
No single person, family, or small group has the power to
plunge the country into chaos as Jiang Qing and the Gang of
Four did.

Corruption, especially at the local level, remains a concern, as it causes dissatisfaction and undermines legitimacy. Chapter 6 will explore how corruption is a problem that needs to be fixed, but is not serious enough to cause revolution. There is also no focus on a single ruling family, onto which the entire population might vent. They might dislike the system, but with over 60 million Party members, nearly everyone in the nation has a friend or family member who makes up part of the bureaucracy.

The government sometimes overreacts to potential threats of instability. To Americans, especially those with a limited knowledge of China, these measures can seem brutish. Critics like Richard Burger, a U.S.-based blogger who lived in China for less than three years and who lasted less than a year working for the government mouthpiece newspaper the *Global Times*, wrote on June 26, 2011, on his blog, The Peking Duck, that the government is "a giant squid, tentacles reaching across the nation to restrict all aspects of life in the land it liberated, silencing opposing voices and existing solely for its own perpetuation. Celebrate away, while people who know real freedom snicker . . . and once again [it has] made a laughingstock of itself."

Undercutting Burger's claim that the government is the "giant squid," the nonpartisan, Washington, DC–based think tank Pew Research Center found in 2009 that 86 percent of the Chinese population supports the direction in which the Chinese government is taking the country. In a 2011 survey of 18 countries, the World Health Organization found Chinese are happier overall than any other population, including those in America and France. My own firm's survey results echo those of the WHO and Pew: Chinese are generally happy with most measures implemented by the government.

If government policies were overly harsh, surely they would not garner such a high rate of support. Even if Chinese disagree with certain rules and take issue with widespread corruption, the Chinese people, as tracked by objective metrics, clearly support the overall direction of their government. Support is high not because people are brainwashed or cowed into submission, but because their interests are mostly aligned with the government's goals, and they see how much better life is than during Jiang Qing's reign of terror. Bloggers like Burger are *cultural imperialists,* as defined by Edward Said. Rather than understanding what Chinese people themselves like, they pedantically write off supporters of the government as being apologists, tyrants, or dimwits who just do not know any better.

In 2003, I was sitting in the drawing room of a large Beijing home in one of the main leadership compounds. Next to me was a senior government official, one who is often lambasted in the Western press. He had jet-black hair combed straight back and thick glasses.

We were both peeling oranges and sipping hot green tea. I was a little apprehensive. If this official was as bad as Western critics made him out to be—and rumors about him abound—he might be pure evil. Undoubtedly he was one of the most powerful people I had ever met. Pictures of visiting heads of state hung on the walls behind him.

"Little Mountain," he said, calling me by my Chinese name, "you are American. Can you explain to me why the Western press is always criticizing us no matter what we do?" Before I could answer, he continued. He was used to taking charge and being listened to.

He told me about a concert by the Three Tenors, the name given to Spanish singers Plácido Domingo and José Carreras, and the Italian singer Luciano Pavarotti, when they sang together as a group, that was held in Beijing's Forbidden City. Tens of thousands of people attended the concert.

The Forbidden City is one of China's most important historical places. Emperors lived there. Neighboring it are two of modern China's symbolic administrative infrastructures— Zhongnanhai, where the top officials of the central government work and live; and Tiananmen Square, which is ringed by the country's leading museums. Having the concert in the Forbidden City would be equivalent to having one with tens of thousands of attendees on the White House lawn, with the Washington Monument, Lincoln Memorial, and the Statue of Liberty all relocated there.

A deranged man with a knife started dashing around Tiananmen Square during the concert, trying to stab people and screaming gibberish, the senior official told me. Like any competent police force, the police tackled the lunatic and took him away in a police van. The official told me a major Western newspaper ran a story covering the incident to the effect of, "Heavily armed riot police in Tiananmen Square, the site of the Tiananmen Massacre in 1989 where innocent people were slaughtered and massacred as hulking, brutish soldiers suppressed their drive for freedom of speech, arrested a knife-wielding man who was probably aggrieved by a power-driven government." The last sentence of the article noted that the reason why the man was angry was not confirmed.

The senior official asked whether it would make sense to have a lot of armed security on such an occasion. Wouldn't it make sense to arrest a clearly mentally disturbed man trying to stab people?

He asked what American police would have done. Probably Taser him or bludgeon him with a club before shackling him with handcuffs and throwing him in the back of a police van,

I responded. Nearly a decade later I was proved right, when a New York City policeman pepper-sprayed and manhandled protesters during the Occupy Wall Street protests—yet Western media only criticized that single officer, rather than arguing that the whole political system was complicit.

It obviously pained the senior official to see how China was portrayed in Western media. But he defended his police that day. "Free speech is great, and I want it too, but not if it threatens stability. No one wants to go back to the dark days. Besides, this man was crazy and could have hurt people with his knife."

At the end of the day in China, freedoms that are perceived to have the potential to bring the country back to the repression and destruction of the Cultural Revolution are not considered to be rights, but rather threats.

Even defining freedoms and the threats against them is not quite so black and white. When Westerners discuss basic human rights, the Chinese government (and, in truth, most Chinese people) thinks about a different set of rights. Take freedom of speech, for example. Most everyday Chinese citizens do not care about measures limiting Internet access, which Americans see as a violation of freedom of access to information. Blocking Facebook or Twitter is not enough to drive mass upheaval, because homegrown versions like Sina Weibo or Renren offer equally satisfactory alternatives in Chinese society. The lack of Western alternatives might limit Chinese firms' ability to expand abroad and employ the Internet tools their competitors use, but it won't cause massive internal protests.

Many Americans think there has been little progress in China on freedom of speech. This is not true. Before the 2008 Beijing Olympics, the *Huffington Post* and the BBC's website were blocked, but they are now accessible. Around 500 million Chinese actively access the Internet on a daily basis from computers and mobile phones, making it impossible to stop information flow.

The Chinese government is no longer nervous about letting its citizens travel and study abroad, or view information and content online. Just a decade ago, by contrast, they severely restricted overseas travel to a privileged few.

Now, the government does cast suspicious glances at Web 2.0 social media sites like Facebook and Twitter as possible tools to foment unrest. True, they might be overly concerned but even U.K. Prime Minister David Cameron said during the 2011 London riots he would block and patrol those social media sites being used to stir up violence. There is probably a more elegant solution for China than simply blocking all foreign-run social media sites, but their concerns about how they can be used to foment instability are understandable. Few content sites are blocked today in China, and Chinese can get unfettered access to international news sites that run critical pieces on China's government, like those of the *New York Times*, *TIME*, and *The Guardian*.

In online chat forums, Chinese people constantly criticize government actions, such as the corruption scandals involving high-speed rail investment and overspending on lavish government buildings. There is no shortage of opinions. If you walk down the street in China, it is even common to see people yelling at police who are trying to ticket them for some driving offense or jaywalking. Many Westerners think that the Chinese people are scared to express themselves, and shake with fear when police walk by—but that is simply not true.

The government understands that draconian limits on access to technology would be counterproductive for society, so it has pushed for domestic alternatives like microblogging on Sina Weibo instead of Twitter, and has even encouraged Chinese police to use these channels to communicate directly with the people. These vehicles provide the Chinese with the freedom of speech the West demands for every citizen of the world. The difference between Sina Weibo and Twitter, however, is largely that the government trusts the executives at Sina to delete within minutes a post that may cause unrest, whereas Western-run sites like Google or Twitter will not turn over information if the government legally asks them for it, much as these sites do in America without balking if the Federal Bureau of Investigation provides a warrant.

Younger Chinese might not like curbs on Internet access, or may even think they are silly, but giving up life's comforts and turning to protest is not in their heads. The benefits that the central government brings far outweigh any negatives. They would rather complain about regulations in person and in online chat rooms, and hope that positive changes will be made as officials get less fearful, than try to overthrow the entire political system.

Given the tribulations of the postdynastic era and the impact of the Cultural Revolution, perhaps most Chinese people understand that a Western model of democracy is not necessarily the best system for China now—and potentially never, as Wu Bangguo, currently Chairman and Party Secretary of the Standing Committee of the National People's Congress and ranked second in the Party hierarchy, has stated. Chapters 6 and 10 will further explore reforms in the political system and what a future system might entail, but such a system is more likely to be shaped by Chinese voices rather than Western ones.

Many Westerners view spending on internal stability by the Public Security Bureau to be nefarious—the actions of a Big

Brother–like government—yet do not view the installation of cameras in London, the German government's use of online Trojans to spy on people, or wiretapping in the United States after 9/11 with such fear or anger. Many Chinese see internal security spending as a natural response to new threats to stability. Sometimes people feel certain steps are excessive and a waste of public funds, but nothing serious enough to cause mass unrest. They see progress over recent decades, and understand that for every two steps forward in the reform process, there is one step back.

China is a developing country, evident by the constant reform that government policies undergo. As the government updates them to reflect current conditions, human rights gradually improve, as they need to. There are both noticeable and subtle changes in the right direction, like the skyscrapers that go up yearly and the right to obtain a passport to travel abroad. The skyscrapers indicate the right to do business, something that was not allowed 40 years ago, and acquiring passports and the ability to travel indicate the right to enter and exit the country as one wishes and to learn what lies beyond China's borders.

Fifteen years ago, obtaining a passport was difficult. Now you would be hard pressed to visit any major tourist destination or shopping district in the world without running into scores of middle-class Chinese tourists snapping photos or buying Louis Vuitton bags. Over 50 million Chinese traveled abroad in 2010, and Chinese tourists are now the largest per capita spenders when traveling in France. Contrast this with the situation just several decades ago, when work units dictated marriage, moving within the country was illegal, and divorce was unheard of. For the Chinese people, these freedoms are now all possibilities.

Tangible improvements have created tremendous optimism. People enjoy newfound prosperity and stability, but the Cultural Revolution and its pain are not forgotten, even if it they are not openly talked about. Why dwell on negatives when there are so many positives? They are not blind to the problems plaguing the country today, like corruption, pollution, or income disparities. They do not forgive them either, and constantly pressure the government to address issues more effectively, such as when the food and high-speed train scandals became public. At some point, a deeper analysis of what went wrong during the Cultural Revolution will be needed to ensure that history is not repeated, but for now the wounds and scars are still too raw.

Seeing improvements on a day-to-day basis leads Chinese to strive to improve their own lives alongside their country and to focus on making money. The drive for wealth is a major reason why fewer are willing to toil in factories or sell their bodies. They aspire to reach higher social classes, make money, buy quality premium brands, and make a better life for their families. They want the Chinese version of the American dream.

As Chinese people prosper, and a stable China grows more important on the world stage, understanding how China's recent history and experiences like Lili Li's continue to shape society today and in the future will help us understand what kind of China is emerging and how it will disrupt the world, and will allow foreign businesses and governments to react in time to be on the right side of this development.

I wanted to better understand just how widespread optimism was in China, and how that optimism manifests itself, both in consumption patterns as well as in as family dynamics. So I decided to look deeper into the role of the segment of society that is least understood by Westerners, but that is also the most optimistic part of the population: Chinese women.

CASE STUDIES
WHAT TO DO AND WHAT NOT TO DO IN CHINA

- Emphasize Aspiration in Your Marketing

  Despite 10 percent inflation in food prices in 2011, consumer optimism remains high. Older generations remember the dark days of the Cultural Revolution and are excited by progress. Younger Chinese have never known difficult times and brim with optimism like America's baby boomers in the post–World War II period. They believe China will be the world's next great superpower, and that they, too, are on their way to riches.

  Companies need to decide whether to reposition brands specifically for China to cater to consumer aspirations. For instance, take Pizza Hut's cheap-eats position in America, with plastic utensils and paper plates. In China, Pizza Hut would be unrecognizable to most Americans. Artwork adorns the walls. Seating booths are comfortable and plush, and a focus on top-notch service has made Pizza Hut a destination for dates, business meetings, and special occasions.

  Danish comfort-shoe maker ECCO has also positioned itself as a higher-end brand in China than in U.S. and European markets. The average pair of ECCO shoes sold in China sells for many times more than it does in the West, yet is one of the most popular shoe brands in the country among affluent male consumers. ECCO is positioned as a comfort shoe, but it competes with Gucci for status-seeking consumers. ECCO even sells a $1,000 pair of shoes, and also offers $400 pairs that are popular among companies as gifts for clients.

  Companies like British retailer Marks & Spencer, on the other hand, continue to emphasize their middle-class heritage too much—consumers want either luxury like Louis Vuitton, or affordable value like Zara. No one wants to be middle class in the American or British sense, where upward socioeconomic mobility is difficult. The few Marks & Spencer stores in China remain devoid of high-spending Chinese consumers. Most shoppers at its flagship Huai Hai Road location in Shanghai are foreigners and older Chinese.

Similarly, hypermarket retailer Walmart continues to lose market share to specialty shops in China, because its motto of everyday low prices does not appeal to their main buyers, who tend to be upwardly mobile middle class and wealthy consumers seeking quality and good value rather than a better price. There are always lower prices than Walmart's at roadside stalls and mom-and-pop stores, so positioning itself this way is not a sustainable, long-term strategy. Walmart's market share plummeted to 5.5 percent in 2011 from 8 percent three years earlier as organic fruit shops and other specialty stores took market share.

Key Action Item

Even global brands should consider localizing their image for the Chinese market as food giant Yum! Brands did with all of their subsidiaries. Chinese consumers typically demand more premium products, so brands should follow ECCO and Pizza Hut's leads and go more upscale. It is difficult to compete on price with domestic brands that do not adhere to the same international standards as Western brands and that have lower cost structures.

- Never Forget the Primacy of the Party

   The Communist Party does not control every aspect of business and life anymore, but businesses should never forget the primacy of the Party—and the political risk if you do something at odds with the central government's agenda. Take the Internet sector, for instance. It is one of the few major sectors controlled by private enterprises like search engine firm Baidu and social media company Tencent, rather than by large, state-owned conglomerates, because of their ability to move fast, respond to trends, and understand consumers.

However, the government will crack down on the Internet sector in order to ensure it follows the goals of the Party. Companies need to make sure their offerings appeal to consumers as well as the government. During sensitive times, the government will shut websites or force companies to increase oversight, which adds to their costs.

Key Action Item

Companies need to perform double the operational due diligence they would do in more market-oriented economies. Ensure the market demands your products or services, but also that the government supports development of that industry, especially by foreigners. If the market wants something but the government does not, companies selling it will fail.

- The Older Generation

  Consumers over the age of 60 are part a lost generation. They never made serious amounts of money because of the turmoil of the Cultural Revolution. If they worked in state-owned enterprises, they also were forced to retire at age 50 for women and 55 for men. Life spans are now 74.8 years for women and 71.3 for men, according to the United Nations. These people stretch out limited pensions over decades. They have 60 percent savings rates, are extremely price sensitive, and rely on children for purchasing products. It is common to see hundreds of older people lining up at Carrefour for specials on eggs or cooking oil.

  Older Chinese also are unaware of brand identities, having grown up in a period where there were few foreign brands. The only brands they used when coming of age were state-owned brands that mostly have disappeared.

  Yet companies should not neglect the older generation. With weak medical-care coverage, older generations seek medical solutions outside of hospitals, and they are part of family trips and family living arrangements. They influence decision makers even when they do not pay.

Their children, very typically people in their thirties, make the purchasing decisions for older generations. Target younger Chinese and convince them to buy items for their parents and grandparents. Family duty and obligation is ingrained, and in many cases is stronger than in Western markets, where older generations often prefer to make decisions themselves.

Key Action Item

Decision makers in China are often different from the decision makers in the West, making the value chain longer and more complicated. Brands need to understand who the influencers are in the purchasing process, and who makes the final decision, to properly target buyers.

- Young Buyers

  The average age of Mercedes Benz buyers in the United States is 53; in China it is 39. Target markets are generally far younger in China than in other nations, because younger executives seized opportunities after reforms began in 1978. Position your brands and launch advertising campaigns geared to younger consumers by incorporating different marketing images and communication channels than those you would use in America or even Japan.

  Bentley buyers, for instance, are often thirtysomething, Internet-savvy entrepreneurs. They are more likely to buy sportier and faster Bentleys than their counterparts in America. Movie stars, older tycoons, and trust fund babies who buy Bentleys in America do not exist in China. Rampant piracy of DVDs and CDs has made it difficult for Chinese celebrities to make as much money as Western ones unless they perform live concerts or win product endorsements to supplement earnings.

Few of China's wealthy citizens inherited their money, and older tycoons are outnumbered by younger ones.

Bentley has adjusted by pushing a younger, sportier image in its marketing campaigns, and they have benefited from understanding their target markets. China became Bentley's second-largest market in 2011, with over 25 percent of global market share.

Key Action Item

Brand managers need to understand that target markets are far younger in China than in other markets, and they must adjust advertising images and marketing communication strategies for this younger demographic

4

THE MODERN CHINESE WOMAN

I first met Amy back in 1997 when I was living in Tianjin, a port city of 10 million two hours east of Beijing. There were probably only about a hundred foreigners living there then, many of them working at the big Motorola plant that had just opened. Crowds of dirt- and sweat-stained, rural migrant workers who had come to the city to find jobs would follow me around, as one of the few foreigners, and shout, "Hello!" They would be grouped together on roadsides, holding up "job wanted" signs with their skills scrawled on cardboard, when they would see me and come running.

One middle-aged man, whose clothes were so blackened by grime I wondered if they were his only set, approached me and said excitedly I was the first foreigner he had ever spoken to. He must have been dirt poor—I could see his ribs sticking out from underneath his shirt, and he stank—but he was so excited to meet me, he insisted on treating me to a meal of crispy duck followed by unfiltered cigarettes so strong they burned my throat.

I used to love biking through Tianjin's leafy boulevards, lined with the old mansions that Europeans had erected over a century before during the waning days of the Qing Dynasty. The buildings were a welcome contrast to the drab, crumbling, Soviet-style block housing that made up the rest of the city. I would often eat my meals on one of those streets at Broadway Café, one of the few restaurants in the city that served Western food.

Amy was a waitress at Broadway Café. She was petite, with short-cropped black hair and a bashful, mousy demeanor—she looked like she might scamper away just for being talked to. She was clearly someone who had been taught to keep her head down and blend into the background for most of her life. Over the next several years that I saw her at Broadway's, I only exchanged a few words with her beyond asking for more water or French toast. I don't think she ever looked me in the eye. She seemed to change very little from year to year. When I finally left Tianjin for good in 2001, I said good-bye to her, got a quick curt smile in response, and never thought about her again.

Nearly a decade later, I was back in Tianjin on a business trip. I was walking around my old neighborhood, marveling at how completely the place had been transformed. The old block housing was gone, replaced by fancy modern restaurants, shops, and towering skyscrapers. As I wandered around, I heard someone call out my name. I turned around and found myself suddenly being grabbed in a tight embrace.

At first, I didn't recognize the woman in her late twenties hugging me. I looked closer and realized it was Amy. In place of that plain, bashful young girl I remembered stood a beaming, confident young woman, decked out in expensive makeup, toting a designer bag, and sporting a salon-styled hairdo.

Looking at the stylish girl standing in front of me, a decade of change crystallized right in front of my eyes. Instead of the meek waitress with whom I made awkward, limited conversation in that Tianjin restaurant just 10 years before, I was now looking at a polished and self-assured businesswoman.

Later that night, Amy and I went to restaurant after restaurant while catching up. In many ways I was getting to know her for the first time. "Life is so good," Amy said, grinning. Since I had last seen her, she had left her waitressing job and had taken a series of jobs at several of the multinational firms that were flooding into the city, and was now thinking about starting her own firm. "The time is now or never to be an entrepreneur," she said. "I don't know what I'll do yet, but I will do something." Amy smiled, fueled by self-confidence and her parents' full-hearted support of her newfound business acumen.

After the Cultural Revolution and the arrest of the Gang of Four, the government concentrated at first on creating wealth and improving gender equality in order to promote stability. This approach was smart for two reasons. First, wealth creation makes it a lot easier for people to stop dwelling on the suffering they faced in earlier years, and less likely to push for violent change. Second, countries that push for gender equality generally develop more quickly and foster more vibrant economies and cultures.

During the Cultural Revolution, being labeled a capitalist was a heinous crime, as Deng Xiaoping and his paralyzed son knew all too well. Now that notion has been turned upside down. People who are not making money are too often looked down on because they lack ambition, potential, and social status. In many cases, the drive to make money has resulted in excesses, including many unscrupulous businessmen who lie, cheat, and cut corners as they try to get rich. Many Shanghainese girls told me they would not even consider marrying someone who has not already bought a house (without a mortgage) and car.

An electric business climate is pulling and pushing everyone to pursue money. Everyone knows someone, or maybe even has a relative, who was formerly a peasant raising pigs or tilling rice paddies covered in night soil, but who now drives a Mercedes and owns multiple villa-style townhouses. Fifteen years ago you only needed $6 million in total assets to make the top 100 on the *Forbes* China Rich List; last year the mark was $120 million. There are now several hundred billionaires in U.S. dollar terms in China—all self-made—and over one million millionaires. *The Hurun Report* estimates there are more billionaires in China than in the United States. I personally know about eight people who were barely scraping by to survive two decades ago, but who are now billionaires. With all the dizzying wealth creation around them, everyone feels like they, too, can make it big and achieve their dreams.

Rapid growth has driven Chinese women to break out of their formerly subservient roles and reach parity with men in society's eyes. In Amy's case, she went from meek waitress to savvy business-woman to fledgling entrepreneur. As we left a restaurant that evening, where we had chatted easily, Amy told me to keep in touch and suggested that we "do some business deals together soon."

Prior to my first trip to China, my image of Chinese women had been limited to portrayals in movies like *The Last Emperor* or *The Joy Luck Club,* and by stories of the travails of women recounted to me by relatives on my mother's side of the family, whose ancestors had left southern China in the 1840s to work on the railroads in California. My family had never actually been to the mainland, but they told me all the horror stories that had been passed down from generation to generation about the plight of women.

When I first arrived in Beijing, I half-expected women to be concubines with bound feet who were treated like chattel— or at least downtrodden, like the women I had heard my relatives talk about. I had read lots of newspaper articles about the male–female gender imbalance to prepare for my trip, but there's not much objective literature or general knowledge in the West about China's current culture, or what the role of women there is really like. Reading current depictions in Western media of women in China, it is difficult to envision a forward-looking society led by powerful women. The Japan-based Bloomberg columnist William Pesek argues that Chinese society "neglects" women and that there is rampant gender discrimination. As proof, he points to the fact that only two women have been appointed governors in China, while Americans have elected 32 during the same time period.

When you see firsthand how the role of Chinese women has changed since the mid-1990s, however, it is clear that the idea of the modern Chinese woman is the opposite of images like those in *The Last Emperor,* and that analysts like Pesek are holding onto and perpetuating outdated notions of women's role in Chinese society.

Female empowerment has somewhat paradoxically been accelerated by the implementation of the one-child policy, introduced in the late 1970s to curb runaway population growth. It is true that the one-child policy has caused sex-selective abortions and outright female infanticide in rural areas, where the importance of strong bodies and hands for farm labor has created a powerful preference for boys. This policy has also helped result in a male–female imbalance of 118 to 100, often much higher in rural areas. Some estimate that there are 30 million more men of marrying age than women.

However, for years the government has been taking several steps to combat infanticide through such measures as banning doctors from reporting a child's sex to expectant parents, and allowing parents to have two children in some parts of the country if the first child is female. They have also allowed women to initiate divorce; likewise, arranged marriages are a rarity now.

In urban China, where physical strength is no longer needed to support the family, girls are as welcome as boys. All the hopes, dreams, and aspirations of parents and grandparents, whose lives were disrupted by the Cultural Revolution, are placed on girls, who are raised as little princesses. Women are now viewed as just as capable—if not more so—as their male counterparts of performing highly on achievement tests and ultimately becoming the breadwinners of the family in the workforce. This shifting mentality has caused male–female ratios in urban areas to draw closer to the worldwide norm, which is 107 males for every 100 females, according to the Central Intelligence Agency.

Many couples still bribe doctors to disclose information about the child's sex, especially in rural areas, but the preference for boys is even beginning to decline there as well. China's urbanization rate rose above 50 percent for the first time in 2010, up from 30 percent just a decade earlier. As a result, strong hands for farming are no longer as prized as they once were. Additionally, the government has made establishing better social security and medical care access for rural communities a priority, which further lessens elderly people's notion that they need sons to help care for them as they become infirm.

In the past three years, when interviewing migrant families in major cities like Beijing and Shanghai, I discovered an even more surprising trend: Female migrants often outearn their male counterparts. More women are starting to work in service industries, taking jobs like waitressing and house cleaning, where salaries tend to be higher than in physical-work-based jobs like construction and recycling.

In the 1950s, the first decade after the Communists came to power, Chinese women accounted for only 20 percent of household income. In the nineties, when I first met Amy, they accounted for 30 percent. Now women account for more than half of income, and there are now more women in university than men. Women account for 55 percent of the $15.6 billion of luxury items bought by mainlanders in 2011, and *Forbes* reports that 7 of the world's 14 self-made billionaires are Chinese women.

Research suggests Chinese women enjoy working, and are not willing to stay at home. In many cities like Shanghai, couples who are themselves both only children are allowed to have two children rather than just one. A survey conducted by the Guangzhou-based magazine *New Weekly*, however, found that 81 percent of eligible couples countrywide wanted just one child; only 14.5 percent said they wanted two. The main reasons were that they were worried about the high costs of raising two children, and how having two children would influence the couple's career development. The Shanghai Academy of Arts and Sciences found that 45 percent of Shanghainese couples did not want a second child.

Positive trends toward gender quality, accompanied by the hard facts on the ground, all add up to one thing: Chinese women are becoming empowered in the workplace, and their changing role in family dynamics, especially rural families, has had more impact on Chinese society than is understood by most Westerners.

Amy is typical of the generation of Chinese women born in the late 1970s and early 1980s that shifted from being meek girls to confident, aggressive consumers and entrepreneurs. By contrast, Melanie, a young woman born and raised in China, is a good example of an urban woman born in the late 1980s and early 1990s.

Melanie and I were sitting next to each other on one of the newly opened high-speed trains connecting Nanjing and Shanghai that cut travel time in half and increase business productivity. She was tall, and had an athletic build, long, sculpted legs, and a bouncy smile. The train was so crowded that her leg pressed against mine, while an old man on my other side practically had his arm in my lap.

I had planned to spend the train ride reading, when Melanie struck up a conversation. She began telling me about her family and her career goals. Her body language showed she was at ease opening up to a foreigner—she had none of the shy nervousness that Amy had when she was a waitress at Broadway in Tianjin.

Melanie told me her mother was denied the chance to go to college because the university system closed during the Cultural Revolution. By the time universities reopened in the 1980s, her mother was already too committed in her career working at a state-owned enterprise to go back to school. She also missed out on profiting from the great economic reforms that were going on, because she was too unsophisticated to open her own business. She remained mired in a low-level position in her company until she lost her job in the late 1990s, as tens of millions of other people did when the government cut state-owned enterprise jobs to move to a more market-oriented economy.

Melanie's mother had married not out of love, but because her husband was labeled as an appropriate, marriageable candidate by the Chinese government due to his family background. Permission from the government was needed in those days to marry. Over the years, Melanie's mother had come to accept her husband, but like so many Chinese families in her generation, marriage was more a pact for shelter and support than a match made out of love.

As Melanie described the pressures her parents put on her, I saw in many ways her mother was living vicariously through Melanie. She pushed Melanie to get a master's degree so her daughter could have the education she had missed, and to gain Communist Party membership to benefit from opportunities. Finally, she pushed Melanie to marry for love rather than security. Melanie's father virtually ignored her mother; he showered Melanie with boundless love and support.

Melanie's remarks of how her mother and father behaved resonated with my own experiences. When nightclubs first started opening up in China, club-goers were usually not young people, but middle-aged men and women dressed up in revealing clothes as if they were 20-year-olds, dancing on the floor with an unnatural ferocity. It always seemed to me they were trying to capture a past they had never gotten a chance to experience.

My talk with Melanie showed how clearly the Cultural Revolution still impacts Chinese society across generations. Melanie's mother felt she missed out on her career and a happy home life, so she pushed her daughter to strive for the best and to realize her dreams. She also spoiled her, waiting at home for her every night until she got home from work to make dinner for her. Despite Melanie being in her twenties, her mother still washed all of her clothes.

Outside of work, Melanie had few financial responsibilities or costs. Her parents covered her food and housing expenses. She was so confident of her future career earnings that she did not save any of her $1,000 monthly salary at her entry-level business development job with a consulting company; she spent it all on shopping and eating at restaurants with friends. She had just signed up for a credit card, so instead of having to save up for two months before buying the latest iPhone, she could buy it on credit. She told me she changed her mobile phones every nine months, selling old ones through online e-commerce sites like Taobao.

There are millions of young, upwardly mobile women in China just like Melanie. They are showered with love and are taught to believe they can achieve anything. Their parents are doing whatever they can to help them achieve the goals they had for themselves, but were not able to achieve due to the disruption of the Cultural Revolution. And they are optimistic that their personal and professional lives will continue to get better and better and better.

Most horror stories about China's gender inequality now occur in rural areas. Some villages have 150 boys for every 100 girls, and in these backward places women are still destined to live lives of servitude. Thankfully, as with rising gender equality in urban areas, the inferior status of rural women is starting to change, as salaries for the positions migrant women typically take in the service sector outpace those of men, and as better educational opportunities are introduced.

Julie came from a totally different world than Melanie. I met her one day in Shanghai at a massage parlor. My feet were aching after a long run, and I needed a foot massage to ease the kinks out. Julie was the masseuse assigned to me. As I dipped my feet into a bucket of warm water laced with traditional Chinese medicinal herbs—the first part of a foot massage—Julie started to tell me her life story.

Julie was born in the late 1980s on a rice farm in Jiangxi in south central China, one of the most underdeveloped provinces in the country. Life there was a struggle for everyone when Julie was a child. Access to food often depended on conquering nature. Frequent floods and droughts scourged the area.

Where Julie grew up, 40-year-olds looked like 90-year-olds, as the hard farm work turned skin into leather. Feet were calloused from walking the mountainous terrain without adequate foot-wear, and fingernails were yellow and thick. Luckily for Julie, she was not destined for a life on the farm. She married young, and she and her husband left the countryside alongside tens of millions of other migrants looking for work in urban areas. Through hometown connections, they ultimately both found work in Zhejiang, an industrialized province, at a fashion-accessory factory. There she glued buttons onto accessories destined for America and Europe. Julie soon found a job at a foot massage parlor, and dropped her tiresome job in the factory for the higher-paying position as a masseuse.

Julie later moved to Shanghai, where she now gives mas-sages to between five and seven wealthy Chinese clients a day. Foreigners sometimes come, she said, but Chinese are the bigger spenders. The pay and working conditions in massage parlors are better in Shanghai than in Zhejiang. The work is hard and tiring, and she has huge, yellowed calluses on her knuckles from pressing against her clients' feet, but she makes nearly $700 a month—a fortune in her hometown, where it often takes half a year to make that much.

Unfortunately, Julie's husband couldn't find work in Shanghai, so he returned to Zhejiang, where he makes $200 a month as a worker in the fashion-accessory factory. Julie said it was tough being away from her husband, whom she married for love, but her family needed to make money.

Julie said she recently bought a $90,000 apartment back in her hometown of Jiangxi, using mostly her own earnings as a deposit. She had saved most of her earnings for eight years to put a 20 percent down payment on her home. For the vast majority of Chinese, owning a home—something that was not allowed in the first four decades of Communist rule—has a profound significance. People do whatever they can to buy a home, and they view it as the ultimate goal in life. They often pool money from parents and grandparents and live together under one roof. The average age of a home buyer in China is 27, five years younger than the average home buyer in America.

Julie's two-year-old daughter still lives back in her hometown and is being raised by her husband's parents, so she saves as much of her earnings as possible to send back to them. It is hard being away from her child, she said, but as she started to push acupressure points on my feet, she justified it to me. "I can make more money than my husband," she said. "We have no culture, no education, so I have to do the work because he cannot make much. My plan is to work here for several more years as long as I am young and physically fit, and then I will go home to be with my family. Maybe I will use my savings to open a small clothing shop."

As Julie told me her story, I could hear alternating pride and frustration in her voice. Pride from becoming the main breadwinner in her family and from the respect this position commanded from her in-laws. The frustration was prominent when she spoke about living away from her daughter, and even more so when she explained to me that her husband would shortly be moving back to Jiangxi to be with her.

Practically speaking, Julie said her husband could probably earn almost as much in Jiangxi cobbling together odd jobs as in a factory in Zhejiang, and having at least one parent raise their child is better than none, so they decided he should move back home. Generations of Chinese children have been raised by grandparents over the last two decades, so parents in their twenties can find better jobs in cities, to work in factories like Laura Furniture's in Guangdong. Sadly, these parents can often only afford to return home during the Chinese New Year holiday.

Job prospects are improving in rural hometowns, so one parent often moves back home to be with the child, like Julie's husband. Construction in particular is slowing in first-tier cities like Shanghai and Beijing, and starting to accelerate in rural areas, so men are finding more construction jobs back in their hometowns. With wages often higher in service sectors that attract women, men are increasingly the ones returning home while the women stay in cities to earn more money.

Four of the maids who have taken care of my home's affairs tell similar stories. All of them make far more money than their husbands do. One of them, Little Qian, told me that her husband was a scrap metal dealer in Shanghai. He combed garbage areas and picked up discarded metal from wealthier housing compounds for recycling. In a good month he made a third of what she did—and we provided her housing on top of her pay. Her husband finally decided to move home to Sichuan Province to raise their eight-year-old son, because salaries for the work he could get in his hometown were almost as high as in Shanghai.

Little Qian is barely five feet tall and slight in build. She tires easily. I often wonder what kind of life she would have had if she had been born a few decades earlier, when the economy was largely agrarian. Her value to the household probably would have been low, because she is too small and weak to contribute much in the fields. Although she is a good-hearted person, she has a hooked nose and gray-black buck teeth. She probably would not have been valued by her in-laws for her beauty, and would not have earned her family a big dowry.

In today's China, however, Little Qian has become the main earner for her family, an impossible role for her only decades before. When she returns home for vacations, she always packs up bundles of goodies for everyone in her extended family. When she comes back from her trips home, she excitedly tells us about how happy each relative was to receive this box of cigarettes or toy car or that bottle of cosmetics.

Countless rural women like Julie and Little Qian have become the main wage earners in their families in just the last few years. The job sphere for even rural women is expanding at a very fast pace. Men are increasingly returning home to do what has typically been a female task: raising children. While uneducated men are often limited to low-paying jobs factory or construction jobs, women have expanded their reach and are able to work in restaurants, massage parlors, and other service-oriented jobs like secretarial work in white-collar companies, where pay is higher due to the tight service-labor market.

Women from all regions and all socio-demographic groups are seeing palpable changes in the quality of their lives, and are no longer desperate enough to work as prostitutes or in other degrading jobs. Why should they, when they can make just as much money as a waitress, even if the work is tough?

New job opportunities, better access to education, and more equal positions in family life are creating a modern Chinese woman. No longer trapped in the countryside, where it is difficult to earn subsistence wages, they are working in well-paying jobs that allow them to save and empower them with unprecedented choices when they consume, be it a new house or the latest trends.

Whether it is the waitress-turned-entrepreneur Amy, white-collar businesswoman Melanie, the masseuse Julie, or the maid Little Qian, the modern Chinese woman is using her newfound wealth and position to influence consumption habits and change how brands need to approach the Chinese market. For brands like Laura Furniture, which need to convert factories from focusing on production for export to America to selling into China, or simply for brands looking to offset dwindling growth in America and Europe, understanding how the modern Chinese woman shops is critical. They not only have money, but they influence major household purchases, like automobiles and real estate, that were traditionally the male domain.

Young female shoppers in China are not as price sensitive as many analysts believe. Women tend to be value driven rather than price sensitive, and look for products that confer status. This means women will shop for luxury brands like Louis Vuitton and Gucci despite the hefty price tag, because they feel these well-known brands project an image of high status that makes them feel successful, which is what gives them value. On the other hand, women gravitate toward more affordable brands like Spanish apparel retailer Zara or H&M, because the clothes are comfortable and of good quality, but not too expensive. They also view these brands as a good value.

The importance of product safety and good value to Chinese women is defining the consumption habits of the entire middle class. In many ways, women's rise in Chinese society and their shopping habits have redefined the Western idea of the emerging Chinese middle class. There is a middle class from a socioeconomic standpoint, but far too many analysts attribute to it the same aspirations and shopping characteristics as the American middle class.

Unlike in America, where people are often born into middle-class families and are content with their children staying in this demographic, Chinese women in the middle-income group are optimistic that they can climb even further up the social scale, either because their salaries are rising so quickly or because they expect to become entrepreneurs themselves, like Amy in Tianjin. With this positive outlook, they purchase more freely than more cautious middle-class Americans as long, as they believe they are buying a safe, high-quality product. Put another way, they don't view themselves as middle class, but rather on the way to becoming rich.

They shop in a way that mirrors the shape of an hourglass. They either buy luxury products, or the cheapest products in categories they do not value. Brands positioned in the middle level, like Gap, get lost in the drive for Louis Vuitton or the cheapest items possible.

If there is a drawback to all of the love and attention being showered on Chinese women, it is that many in urban areas are becoming spoiled to a dangerous extent. Part of the problem is that parents who suffered during the Cultural Revolution don't want their daughters to go through any hardship. They indulge their little princesses, rather than help them learn how to overcome any obstacles they might face on their own.

When the going gets tough, many parents teach their daughters it is better to get going and to run away from difficulties. When a job gets too hard or the hours too long, parents often support the mentality of quitting the job and finding another, perhaps in a state-owned enterprise where salaries are high and hours short. In interview after interview with multinational executives in China, I heard complaints about all of the otherwise bright and talented young Chinese women—and men, in many instances—who were unwilling and unable to tackle serious challenges. At some point decades from now, their lack of grit and determination to overcome challenges, and their willingness to take on debt, might cause China to face some of the same challenges that America is now.

The empowerment of women is one of the great developments of modern Chinese society, and is a further factor in the End of Cheap China. Women are becoming the key drivers of spending; they are beacons of optimism in the country, and a major force behind China's transition toward becoming one of the biggest markets in the world. Western brand managers need to change their outdated notions about who the modern Chinese woman is and what she wants. Chinese companies are already starting to understand these powerful consumers, and are improving their brands to appeal to their values.

CASE STUDIES
WHAT TO DO AND WHAT NOT TO DO IN CHINA

- Think Cute, Not Sexy

  Targeting younger Chinese women between the ages of 24 and 32 is smart, because they drive China's retail sales growth. However, do not forget to take local consumer preferences into account. Mattel launched a 36,000-square-foot, six-story Barbie flagship store in Shanghai that did not cater to Chinese women who often like different styles than Western women. Mattel hired Patricia Fields of *Sex and the City* fame to design clothes for Chinese women. These designs were too sexy; the low-cut blouses showing cleavage put off young women. Many told us they found the clothes "too sexy and revealing" and too expensive for frilly products.

  Chinese women like "cute"; think Hello Kitty rather than sexy. Snoopy-branded clothing is one of the hottest brands for twenty-something Chinese women. Barbie, by contrast, shut its $37 million store two years after opening.

Barbie targeted the right age group, as younger women are the most optimistic group in China and have increasing disposable income, but they failed to that realize young Chinese women are immature relative to Westerners, which is why they like cuter objects. Chinese women often live at home until marriage, and are treated like little princesses, with parents cooking and washing clothes for their daughters even after they have entered the workforce full time.

Key Action Item

Target younger Chinese women between the ages of 24 and 32, but localize for consumer preferences. Companies cannot just bring what worked in the West into China. Understand that Chinese women tend to be more immature and spoiled than Western women.

- Craft Marketing Messages and Use Models to Which Chinese Women Aspire

  Fueled by taking on a larger role in the economy, Chinese women aspire to a life of luxury and personal indulgence. They increasingly have the money to buy global brands to display their aspirations. Marketing campaigns need to use the models and lifestyle aspirations that Chinese women dream about. Brands like Ralph Lauren and Brooks Brothers have made the mistake of using too many blond-haired, blue-eyed female models, summering in Hamptons-like backgrounds, in their advertising campaigns.

  As one 26-year-old Shanghainese women told me, "The models look great, but Western women's hips and busts are different from Chinese. I just do not think I could ever wear those clothes." Ralph Lauren should have used Chinese models that show how Chinese can look in the clothes, and imagery to which Chinese can better relate.

L'Oréal, on the other hand, has chosen female and male models with whom Chinese consumers can identify. The cosmetics giant uses Western models to show its global brand status and heritage, but it also uses Asian models to show that the products are not just for Western women and men with different skin types. China has become L'Oréal's third-largest market globally.

Key Action Item

Companies with premium and luxury positioning should use foreign models to emphasize brand heritage, because Chinese associate foreign brands with quality. But they should also use local models to show how Chinese could truly aspire to that lifestyle, and to show respect.

- Chinese Often Have Different Payment Habits

  While splitting bills is common in America, in China it is far more common for one person, often a male, to pay for everyone. This is even true for teenagers, among whom one person takes charge to show status.

  To facilitate ordering, restaurant chains should have more group-dining menus and set options, so that one person can order and get enough different variety for everyone to enjoy. This will speed up the ordering process, and give restaurants the chance to up-sell by adding more expensive items and those that diners typically will not order for themselves. Savvy domestic Chinese chains like Ye Shanghai, Southern Barbarian, or Xiao Nan Guo heavily push set menus and are able to up-sell.

  Similarly, women prefer to pay on delivery for many purchases, because they are fearful that they will get cheated by unsavory vendors who have one item in a showroom or online, and then switch that with an inferior-quality product at delivery.

Retailers should either allow for consumers to pay cash on delivery or with debit cards (especially if the deliveryman is not trusted or from a third-party logistics firm). If you are a big, trusted brand, then you can charge a deposit, but you will have to give guarantees to your customers.

Key Action Item

Companies need to learn who is paying for their products and services, and how that person likes to pay. Understanding who pays, and creating options for that payer to order quickly and gain status, is a way to generate more revenue per ticket and speed up ordering processes.

- VIP Loyalty Programs Are Important, but Most Are Terrible

     Many analysts say Chinese are not brand loyal. That might have been true a decade ago, when Chinese were first becoming consumers and wanted to try different products and brands to see what fit them. Now loyalty is starting to gain hold, especially among women. One of the best ways to create loyalty with consumers is to develop outstanding VIP loyalty programs.

     One of the most frequent demands that consumers have across many product categories, they tell us, is that they want to be recognized for their loyalty. Yet at the same time, one of the greatest levels of consumer dissatisfaction comes from weak loyalty programs that do not offer buyers what they want.

     Far too many loyalty programs just push discounts or points to get ice cream cones. Many outsource programs to credit card companies, which issue standard awards that these companies use for all their cobranded credit cards. Other brands allow their regional distributors to develop their own programs by province, which creates anger and confusion among consumers who travel throughout the country to shop.

One female Beijing consumer told me about how her favorite footwear brand disenfranchises her. "It is ridiculous. I buy this brand of shoes in Beijing and I get points or a discount from them, but when I go to Shanghai they have a different set. The loyalty program is based on the retailer itself, rather than the brand. I am loyal to the shoe brand, not the retailer."

Instead, brands should use loyalty programs to introduce consumers to products and services from their specific company. Middle-class and wealthier consumers overwhelmingly tell us they do not want pure discounts from loyalty programs, but special products and services, or co-branding projects, that make them feel special.

Key Action Item

Brand managers should spend money and time developing strong programs that do not just rely on discounting to attract female consumers. Programs should be comprehensive and make consumers feel special and valued by the brand.

5

WHY CHINESE CONSIDER KENTUCKY FRIED CHICKEN HEALTHFUL

CHINA'S IFFY FOOD SUPPLY CHAIN IS PUTTING A PREMIUM ON SAFE FOOD

I was interviewing Emily, a twentysomething Shanghainese girl, about her eating habits. Emily had flowing black hair and shapely shoulders, and carried herself with the self-assurance of someone who has been told she could be a model and knows it. She wore a stylish dark-blue dress that matched her looks, mottled brown pumps, and a bright pink Hello Kitty wristwatch. She drank a Frappuccino while she constantly messaged her friends on her iPhone 4, when she suddenly said to me, "I love Kentucky Fried Chicken. I go there all the time because it's healthy." I did a slight double take. Since when is KFC considered healthy?

I pressed Emily to explain. She said, "I know fried food isn't really healthy, but I trust KFC to be safe." I asked her what she meant. "First, I trust that KFC uses real cooking oil," she said. "Lots of street vendors use recycled oil from sewers. I don't think KFC would do that. And they wouldn't put cardboard in their batter—I heard some dumpling restaurants do that to save money. And I don't think they would use expired or tainted ingredients. Many restaurants dye their food or add all kinds of additives that are toxic."

The more Emily and I talked, it became clear she did not consider Kentucky Fried Chicken and other fast food chains like McDonald's and Dunkin' Donuts "healthy" in the conventional sense. She knew fatty, oily foods could cause heart disease as well as a host of other problems, like diabetes. But she saw Western fast food options as offering safer food than many local restaurants. She worried that unscrupulous businessmen, farmers, and restaurant owners would cut corners on safety to make a few extra bucks, so she preferred to dine in foreign-owned restaurants or big domestic chains like Babela's Kitchen, because she trusted they would not use poor-quality ingredients. Emboldened and enriched by better educational and work opportunities, as outlined in Chapter 4, young women like Emily have the money and sophistication to demand better-quality food, and they are willing to pay higher prices for safer and more healthful food options. The trend toward spending more on food is a trend that companies cannot ignore. They must build trust with consumers and offer premium healthful options.

In 2011, my firm interviewed 2,000 Chinese consumers in eight cities about their dining habits. We found that Emily's response actually was not unusual. After years of food scandals hitting the nation's food supply chain—such as the dairy scandal in 2008, in which tens of thousands of babies were sickened from infant formula tainted with melamine—my firm's research suggests many Chinese trust Western fast-food brands like KFC because they believe they would not cut corners in the supply-chain process. Like Emily, they all know that a healthy diet should not include too much oil, meat, or fat, but they often view Western fast-food companies as safer alternatives to local restaurants. Because many consumers lead busier work lives and have more money to spend on leisure, eating at home and cooking their own meals has become less commonplace. We also found they will pay a premium when buying food from trusted sources, especially food destined for children.

It is not hard to see why Chinese consumers are so fearful about eating toxic or contaminated food. Stories abound in newspapers and online forums of local farmers, restaurants, and supermarkets selling expired meat, injecting additives to make pork look like beef, mislabeling products, and even pumping watermelon and other fruits with dirty water to make them heavier. One woman told me that her mother bought ready-to-eat shrimp that she thought looked nice and pink, but she washed them in a pot to be safe, just in case the shrimp were a little dirty. To her horror, dye began leaking from the shrimp into the water and turned it pink. She threw the shrimp out, scared of what their quality might be and what other chemicals might have been added.

One of the surer signs that there are serious problems with the food supply chain is that most people with direct industry experience are even more cautious than laypeople. I once told my local fruit vendor that I like to eat apples without peeling them, and she looked at me like I was crazy, even when I told her I scrubbed the skin with fruit soap. She told me if I saw how farmers grew produce, and what kind of chemicals they spray on them, I would never think about eating the skin again. She said farmers used the cheapest chemicals possible, which are frequently deadly to humans as well as to bugs and bacteria, and often colored the fruit to make it more appealing.

A senior, China-based executive at one of the world's largest hypermarket chains told me to be very careful about what I eat. He said his company spends millions of dollars ensuring safety and teaching farmers proper ways to handle food. "Some of the hygiene practices farmers use is sickening," he told me. "They just don't know how to keep produce clean. They use chemicals to kill bugs. They either do not know or do not care if the chemicals can also kill humans. They often do not clean processing areas enough, so they are basically breeding grounds for bacteria." Instead of taking tea in restaurants, the hypermarket executive told me he carries his own bags of tea imported from abroad everywhere he goes, because he is not sure how clean the tea leaves used in restaurants are.

China's food supply chain is clearly a mess that is literally poisoning the Chinese population. It is causing global fears and a backlash because China plays such a critical role in the global food supply chain. Many processed foods lining the aisles of U.S. supermarkets contain some ingredients that began their journey in China.

Concerned about the scope of the problem, and the anger welling up in the domestic population and throughout the world, the government has even given fairly free rein to the state-owned media to uncover issues and help press for change. Newspapers chronicle problems in restaurants or in dairies nearly every day.

Smarter companies are taking advantage of these fears by investing millions to ensure better oversight of the supply chain. They seek to build trust with consumers by offering safe food and to guarantee they never do anything to damage that trust. McDonald's, for instance, has invested millions to be sure they have an adequate supply of the tasty but healthy potatoes they use for their French fries.

In a survey of 5,000 consumers in 15 cities, my firm found that food and product safety were far and away Chinese consumers' biggest concerns in life. The vast majority of respondents were more worried about these factors than being able to pay for medical bills or their children's education. Moreover, if they had the money, they would be willing to pay 20 percent more for trustworthy brands of any type of product that they or their families might ingest (or could inhale, like paint or varnish on furniture). Many even told us they preferred to buy furniture products from Scandinavian furniture retailer IKEA, because they believed it would use good-quality glue and varnish that would not hurt throats and lungs if the smell were inhaled.

China's government understands the dangers of the crisis of trust in the country's food supply chain, and has made fixing it a priority. The government has urged consolidation in the supply chain, and premier Wen Jiabao has pushed for more farmer's markets to cut its length, because the longer it is, the more likely that problems will occur.

Many of the food-supply problems are so entrenched that progress is slow despite public demand. Major changes are being driven by restaurant chains like McDonald's and Kentucky Fried Chicken, and supermarket chains like Carrefour, which see the need for reliable food sources, and are rushing to improve direct oversight to cater to consumer demands. They know that by offering trustworthy products they can gain loyal customers and charge more.

Chinese consumers increasingly have the income, the sophistication, and the demand for healthy and safe products. Brands should be forewarned that consumers are very unforgiving of those that become associated with tainted products.

One good example is Ajisen Ramen, a Chinese-owned, Japanese-style noodle chain that is one of the most popular restaurant brands in the country, with nearly 600 outlets. In 2011 Ajisen came under heavy criticism after it was alleged that staff used flavor packets to prepare the broth for its soup noodles rather than boiling pork bones, as Ajisen claimed in advertisements it always had. Until the scandal, consumers told my firm one of the main reasons they ate at Ajisen was that they thought quality standards were higher than at most mom-and-pop noodle shops, and that it used safer ingredients.

After the scandal, Ajisen's stock price took a beating, dropping more than 40 percent at one point, as investors feared consumers would shun the outlets. The company's chief executive officer, Poon Wai, was rumored to have lost over $100 million when the share price fell. It would have been much cheaper, both for him and the company, to live up to the standards it had claimed in its ads in the first place. Now Ajisen will have to spend millions to rebuild trust with consumers, and it will take a while for the share price to rebound—if it ever does.

Dozens of Walmart executives in Chongqing were detained in October 2011 when it was found they were mislabeling organic meat. The local government shut 13 stores for two weeks. Yet one Beijing woman told me, "If Walmart as a trusted foreign brand breaches trust like that, I am scared to think about what local retailers do."

The demand for better-quality food from Chinese consumers will also strain global commodity markets and add to worldwide inflationary pressures. If you look at a globe, you will see China is a big country. Really big. It has a slightly larger land area than the United States, including Alaska and other territories, but the scary part is that only 7 percent, or around one million square kilometers of it, is arable. Much of the country is desert and mountains that make farming impossible. Mind-numbing pollution and urbanization are depleting China's aquifers even further, and are forcing the nation to source more and more of its food from other countries. A nation known the world over for rice has even became a major importer of the white grain, as its farmers convert rice-producing fields to cropland for higher-priced produce and nuts that can be exported to the United States and Europe.

The son of one major military figure told me that he was investing heavily in pistachio and almond farms in Xinjiang. He had the goal of replacing California as a major nut-producing sector.

For some countries and companies, the shift of Chinese diets toward higher protein and calorie consumption represents an opportunity, if they can switch their croplands to raise the produce and meats Chinese want. According to U.S. Department of Agriculture data, China imported over $15 billion in food products from America in 2011, up from $6.7 billion in 2006, and is now the second-largest importer after Canada. Within two decades, as waistlines get bigger, China will likely replace Canada. Already America has become China's largest supplier of agricultural products, according to the state-owned newspaper *China Daily*, as it buys U.S.-grown corn and soybeans. Some analysts expect China's demand for corn from the United States to reach 15 million metric tons within three years.

Chinese demand for U.S.-raised meat products will continue to grow as incomes rise and Chinese get more accustomed to meat-laden diets. Exports of pork to China increased fivefold between 2010 and 2011 to 200 million tons. Right now, Chinese consumption of meat per capita is half of America's—over 125 kilograms per year.

While some companies will benefit from evolving Chinese appetites that demand better-quality food products, problems could emerge as global food supply chains get strained. Speculators from around the world are sitting in cafés to see how many cups of coffee Chinese buy so they can make bets on the coffee bean market. Coffee bean prices hit all-time highs in 2011 largely due to increased demand for coffee from Chinese consumers. Unless technology can keep up with China's growing food demands, it is likely that global food prices will move higher.

For nearly eight years, I regularly ate at what I thought was a Subway sandwich shop located a minute from my office. The shop is in the lobby of a towering skyscraper in the heart of Lujiazui, Shanghai's financial district, and its tenants include the Chinese headquarters for many Fortune 500 firms. Rolls-Royces and Mercedes line its parking lot. The Shanghai Stock Exchange is a 30-second walk away, and two minutes away is the Shanghai World Financial Center, the tallest building in China.

Every day the Subway shop was packed by Western and Chinese executives craving tasty, healthy food and maybe a cookie or pack of potato chips. Sometimes the wait to order was 30 minutes long. The outlet had the exact same menu, signs, and uniforms as every other Subway restaurant in America and China. This shop wasn't a *shanzai*—the term used for obviously fake imitations of famous products or brands you see around China, often with bizarre or comical names like Starbooks, McDnoald's, or Pizza Huh.

No, this was a real Subway restaurant in every perceptible way, with the exception of two minor discrepancies that a reasonable person might assume were the fault of poorly trained staff or maybe a sloppy franchise owner. The first was that instead of wrapping sandwiches in wax paper with the Subway logo, the staff used generic wrappers that simply said, "Good Food." The second was that the cookies always looked slightly flat, as if the bakers had not added enough baking soda to the batter.

I never gave these discrepancies a second thought until, one day, we interviewed a former Subway executive who told us that the sandwich shop was a complete fake. It was opened by unscrupulous entrepreneurs who had set up multiple fake Subways throughout the country. The executive told me that was why the cookies looked different and the daily promotions in that outlet varied from those in others.

Subway corporate headquarters had even sued the owners of the fake Subway several years earlier in a Chinese court, and had won. The court ordered the shop to close and pay a fine. The problem was that there was little enforcement of court decisions, so for years the restaurant kept running without any change. Hundreds of people a day, including me, ate lunch at a fake Subway located at one of the most prestigious addresses in China. Subway kept up the legal pressure, to little effect.

After years of court battles, the restaurant near my office started making subtle changes. For a time the "B" in the SUBWAY sign over the restaurant was blocked out. Once that happened, customers started wondering what was going on. I asked one of the counterpeople, who shrugged and told me the sign was broken. I had my suspicions. When I went to another Subway outlet, the clerk told me that it was a fake Subway.

Employees at the fake Subway papered over other letters in the sign, a new one every month or two—a stalling tactic for the courts, but one that caused concern among more and more consumers. The lines started to thin, and word began to get out that the Subway was actually a fake outlet.

Years later, the restaurant finally took down the sign altogether. Today, the shop still uses menus identical to those at the real Subway located a block away in the Shanghai World Financial Center. The owners changed the sandwich wrappers, though; they now feature a new logo, with lettering practically identical to Subway's but with a slightly different name: Starway.

The brazenness of some of the copying in China is breathtaking. Worse, from a consumer protection standpoint, is the poor enforcement. This business was able to operate for years, despite being found liable by a Chinese court for infringing on Subway's intellectual property.

Contrary to Western opinion, which believes Chinese courts are stacked against Western companies, it is quite common in intellectual property infringement cases for Chinese courts to find in favor of Western brands and order penalties. The problem comes with enforcement—no one shuts down the infracting party. Additionally, many of the laws on the books don't carry adequate punishments. Fines are simply too low to act as a disincentive to counterfeiters; often they pay them and carry on. One lawyer even told me that it was not worth suing a company. His legal fees would be more than the judgment, and anyway it was unlikely that a court order would stop the infringement. It was better to take your case to the consumer, he said, and get them to boycott fakes while buying the real thing.

Where the law failed to stop the fake Subway and shut it down, consumer activism did not. As word got out that the Subway store was actually a fake and not undergoing renovations (this is what staff told customers), fewer and fewer people ate there. Now at lunchtime there are no lines at the sandwich counter, even though the food and prices are the same as two years ago. Consumers do not want to eat food from a fake brand, because they are worried about the safety of the products sold.

I was talking about the shop with a Chinese financial services executive who works in the area. Disgusted and indignant, he said, "If that owner was willing to cheat Subway so much with all their money and lawyers, that owner would be willing to sell me bad-quality food. Who knows what kind of meats they sell? I will never eat there again because the food might harm me." The owner of that fake Subway might have made a lot of money for years by cheating Subway and consumers, but his store is now devoid of consumers, and he is stuck with a long-term lease. Meanwhile, at the Shanghai World Financial Center, the real Subway continues to do brisk business, with lines dozens deep often extending out the door.

How can you trust a restaurant to sell genuinely safe food when penalties for blatantly flouting the law are so light? In an environment with a weak judicial system and unscrupulous food executives, it is little wonder that Chinese consumers have become extremely cautious about what they eat. Many younger people, like Emily, look to KFC and McDonald's to provide food that is at the very least safe, if not exactly healthful.

The same fears about buying expired, tainted, or poor-quality products inform shopping choices at the supermarket. My own personal experience as a parent in China mirrors the problems and fears that many young parents have shared with me. In 2007, after my son Tom was born, I flew to Hong Kong or America every three months to buy baby formula. Back home in Shanghai, my wife Jessica and I bought only imported baby food, even if they were several times more expensive than domestic alternatives, and only at supermarkets like Jenny Lou's (a high-end shop catering to expatriates and wealthy Chinese) that we trusted not to label jars falsely as imports, or to intentionally sell expired or poor-quality products. It was exhausting thinking about not only what food to buy, but also which brands and sales channels I could trust when shopping for my son. The purchasing process became a major topic of conversation between my wife and me at nearly every meal.

My firm's research showed me that many Chinese parents are similarly frustrated, and spend lots of money and time to try and mitigate the chances of giving their children poor-quality food. One Beijing father in his thirties told me that he only shops at the French hypermarket Carrefour because he trusts them to sell only genuine items. "Smaller supermarkets might sell expired goods, or even fake ones," he continued. "You can't just buy based on brand anymore—there are too many fakes. You have to use a trustworthy store as well."

Cross-border baby formula shopping trips like the ones I used to take are now so common that in Hong Kong, it has become nearly impossible for locals to buy formula, because parents from mainland China are always buying it up. Mothers in Hong Kong complained that they often could not find formula for their children, and rules have been implemented to limit the number of cans that one person may buy. I used to spend entire days visiting a well-worn path of stores to restock my son's three-month supply, bumping into other parents from the mainland doing the same thing. Hong Kong police often report arrests after fights break out in stores, as desperate mainland shoppers try to snatch up the last cans.

Hong Kong's Independent Commission Against Corruption reported that 18 people were arrested in May 2011 for skirting the quota on baby formula purchases. Chinese entrepreneurs would work with supermarket staff to buy cans in Hong Kong to ship back to China, to sell through word of mouth or online to Chinese consumers. That's right—desperation for safe food is so high that gangs are moving away from drugs, pirated DVDs, and prostitution to sell baby formula.

When it comes to children and babies especially, Chinese parents are willing to do anything within their budgets to ensure that they are buying something safe and nontoxic. As my wife and I found out, buying baby products in a country with constant product and food safety scandals, involving everything from lead-painted toys to pork masquerading as beef, is a scary prospect.

Many parents—ourselves included—turned to Internet forums in droves to seek advice on trustworthy and nontrustworthy baby-product labels. The problem is that fears are so high, and the market so rife with rumors, that it is hard to know what to trust anymore. A rumor on a microblogging site is enough to destroy a company's reputation and bottom line.

There are dozens of websites enumerating the pros and cons of different brands, and warning against labels that are commonly counterfeited or may be tainted. One mother commenting on a forum warned against buying Nestlé baby formula because she feared the fact that the brand had factories in the northeast, China's rust belt. She worried that pollution from all the heavy industry in the region would seep into the soil and contaminate the grass the cows grazed. Other mothers disagreed, saying Nestlé was trustworthy because it is a foreign brand and therefore less likely to cut corners in the production process than domestic Chinese brands. Some mothers spoke knowingly about certain labels and expiration dates that indicated counterfeit products. As it turned out, these seemingly irrational fears for our newborns were not as crazy as they seemed.

In 2008, a year after my son was born, the whole country was engulfed by the news of a scandal that halted the country's milk supply chain. Thousands of babies became sick due to tainted milk, because unscrupulous people were adding melamine—a chemical that can cause cancer or damage to reproductive systems—to falsify that the dairy products had sufficient levels of protein during quality checks. Sales of imported yogurt shot up as desperate parents feared all dairy supplies produced in China. More parents travelled abroad to buy food if they could afford it. Many switched away from dairy products altogether to soy milk. Breastfeeding became popular again, with some poorer women selling their breast milk to feed babies with wealthier parents.

Despite government efforts to crack down on the dairy supply chain that had produced this catastrophe, finding trustworthy milk in China can still be a harrowing experience. Three years after the original scandal, the government in 2011 shut 50 percent of the dairies because officials were finding that many producers, mind-bogglingly, were still adding melamine. The government has been forcing more consolidation in the industry to ensure better oversight. In August 2011, the government announced it had arrested 2,000 people and shut 4,900 businesses to clean up the food supply chain. Yet that is likely a small drop in a bucket because the problems are so immense.

Safeguarding the food supply chain for export and internal consumption is an area that the Chinese government absolutely needs to work on if it wants to keep the support of the people. It needs to write new laws and enforce them better, or else confidence in and support for the government will wane. Hefty fines and jail terms as well as capital punishment need to be increased to serve as real deterrents. Situations like the fake Subway operating for years despite a judicial ruling against it can no longer be allowed, and simple fines are not enough.

Part of the problem is that laws set by the central government are not always carried out by local officials, because of outright corruption or inefficiency. Far too often, local officials are not arrested or sacked en masse. Instead, the government metes out a severe sentence to senior officials in the hopes of scaring the entire bureaucracy. That strategy rarely works, so a more broad-based and transparent enforcement system needs to be implemented to stop problems and regain consumer confidence in the food supply chain.

These problems, however, provide opportunities for market-oriented brands that understand the evolving Chinese consumer to launch supply chains and marketing campaigns that engender trust. They must never do anything to harm their reputation, as Ajisen and Walmart did, and they need to spend more money up front to ensure safety. Their initial investments will pay dividends in the long term with profits and brand loyalty.

Chinese dairy brands like Mengniu and Yili have already responded to the demands of the market. They understand the need to prove to their customers that their supply chains are safe, and they are investing heavily to modernize their production facilities and advertise these improvements. That is why Mengniu is charging more for their yogurt products than foreign brands: to emphasize their high quality. Western fast-food brands such as KFC understand that consumers like Emily patronize them because they trust their quality control as much as the food's taste. Their advertising campaigns emphasize health to allay consumers' fears about dining out and then dying from eating toxic products.

Consumer demand for better quality is forcing companies to end the practice of a Cheap China. Financially it is more beneficial to sell healthy and safe products at a premium, than to focus on cutting costs at the expense of product quality.

CASE STUDIES
WHAT TO DO AND WHAT NOT TO DO IN CHINA

- Emphasize "Safe" and "Nontoxic"

  Chinese women are petrified of buying toxic products for themselves and their families. In interviews with 5,000 consumers in 15 cities, my firm found that Chinese women are more concerned with product safety than paying medical bills or for their children's education. Every day, China's newspapers abound with a new product or food scandal that heightens fears. From producers adding melamine to the dairy supply to falsify protein levels, to restaurants dyeing food or using swill cooking oil (oil scavenged from sewers, or leftover and untreated from previous uses), Chinese women are scared of buying products that can harm their health.

  Our research suggests they will pay premiums for brands and products they trust to obtain safe and healthy products. Branding is not enough, however, as fears of buying counterfeit or expired products in stores remain a big concern, too. Brands must focus on building trust through the product and brand itself, but must also develop trusted sales channels. For instance, the Lotus supermarket chain, a large Thai group, boasted to me that it even gives seeds to farmers to ensure quality control. Other brands, such as Amway, rely on door-to-door selling because consumers trust buying from neighbors or relatives more than from unknown salespeople.

Companies need to build trust and avoid doing anything to jeopardize their brands. Take luxury furniture retailer Da Vinci furniture, a Singapore-founded and Shanghai-based company that sells Versace Home, Fendi Casa, Kenzo Maison, and Cerruti, among other upscale brands, to wealthy Chinese consumers. Their products often sell for tens of thousands of dollars apiece.

Despite Da Vinci's high prices, reporters from the state-owned CCTV media group described in an exposé that they found quality problems with the company's products. The Shanghai Entry-Exit Inspection and Quarantine Bureau announced that some of the company's "Made in Italy" products were actually made in China. The products were shipped to China's border, and then suddenly became "imported" the next day after local officials had been bribed to certify them as imported—or "Made in Italy."

Da Vinci's reputation was destroyed when their unsavory business practices came to light. In a country fearful of buying poor-quality products, it will cost Da Vinci millions at a minimum to try to repair customers' trust. It is not a foregone conclusion that they will be able to continue their operations.

Key Action Item

Marketing campaigns must build trust and emotional connections with consumers and emphasize safety and use of nontoxic materials. Companies should avoid doing anything to damage that trust, as Da Vinci furniture did. When it comes to health and safety, Chinese consumers are unforgiving.

- Tweak Products and Packaging for Chinese Women

Kraft's Oreo line has been one of the biggest success stories for foreign food brands in China. Their recipe for success? They localized their Oreo line to offer single-serving Oreo wafers. Women often prefer the lighter, crispier texture of wafers to harder cookies. The single-serving packages fit the budgets and consumption habits of teenagers looking for a quick snack and women worried about their figures. The wafers are given shelf placement at cash registers, right near gum and candy, becoming impulse purchases for many consumers.

Often, Chinese women have different tastes than foreigners, and these tastes even vary by region. Women in Sichuan like spicier food, while those in Shanghai prefer sweeter products. Not only might Western brands such as Kraft have to localize product tastes, but they might need to introduce different tastes for different regions. For example, Kentucky Fried Chicken sells more spicy chicken meals in Sichuan than in other regions. Frito-Lay sells more of its spicier flavors there, too, but more of their blueberry-flavor products elsewhere.

Key Action Item

Women's budgets and taste in food are often very different in China than in other markets. Brands might need to sell smaller packages for women concerned about their figures—even at the same price per piece—and localize flavors by region.

6

UNDERSTANDING CORRUPTION IN CHINA

WHAT CHINA'S UNDERGROUND SEX TRADE SHOWS ABOUT ITS GOVERNMENT

I was showing my good friend Jack, who was visiting China from the United States, around Shanghai. I hadn't seen Jack in over a decade, since our boarding school days at St. Paul's School in New Hampshire, and it was great seeing him again. Jack is one of those incredibly brilliant people whose talent causes your jaw to drop. He started a hedge fund, runs marathons, and speaks five different languages.

As we walked down the street, he kept blurting out, "There's one, and another one!" I looked over at Jack, who was pointing at the beauty salons with their pink-neon-lit interiors. Inside each one sat dozens of middle-aged, bloated women wearing cheap makeup. The necklines of their tight shirts plunged low, exposing their propped-up cleavage and giving them the appearance of overstuffed, raw sausages.

"I can't believe there are so many brothels!" Jack continued, his brow wrinkling. "How can prostitution be so open?" he asked as he pointed at the elementary school less than 20 yards away on the corner. He found it especially odd because he had read in the news that the Chinese government was holding a morality campaign to crack down on prostitution and pornography. "Wasn't there that college professor in Nanjing that just got busted for organizing orgies online?" He was baffled that there could be such blatant flouting of the law in what he assumed would be a tightly controlled authoritarian state.

With his observation, Jack touched on an issue that goes far beyond the realm of prostitution and deeper into contemporary Chinese society: the divide between the central and local government, and how laws are enforced. It is common for Westerners to think of the China's government as a large, monolithic authoritarian entity. But in reality there are many different parts.

Aside from the central government, there are provincial, county, municipal, and district governments. While technically they are under the central government's authority, they are given leeway in implementing and interpreting national policies. They are all pulling in different directions. Different regions—and different ministries within the government—often have competing and, in some cases, diametrically opposed interests. One needs to analyze different parts of the government through a more nuanced lens to understand how the End of Cheap China increasingly will force the bureaucracy to change.

Despite the central government's attempt to eradicate prostitution—a process aided by the proliferation of better job opportunities, which is lowering the beauty quotient of the average prostitute—finding a hooker, albeit an ugly one, is not difficult in any city in China. All one needs to do is look for pink lights or a salon whose occupants are all just waiting around. Their easy availability confuses many visitors like Jack, who only get their information about the structure and policies of the Chinese government from foreign media sources.

It is true that the central government is always cracking down on prostitution. Every time I pick up a copy of one of the state-run newspapers, I see headlines like:

GOVERNMENT EMBARKS ON ONE-HUNDRED-DAY CRACKDOWN ON PROSTITUTION

Or:

GOVERNMENT SENDS HOOKERS FOR RETRAINING

In some cities it has become popular for authorities to publicly shame prostitutes as part of their punishment, and there are often pictures in the news of large groups of women in correctional uniforms being paraded through town. The government bans pornographic publications entirely, and is generally strict about any sexual content in television programs. Plans to open a Playboy Club in Shanghai were quashed by local authorities for fear of it being too risqué, and television shows like the popular singing competition Super Girl were banned. On the other hand, Jack and I passed over a dozen brothels in under an hour in China's most cosmopolitan city, and in smaller-tier cities business deals are commonly cemented at karaoke clubs and saunas swarming with prostitutes, with hardly any interruption by local authorities. How could this be?

The answer is pretty simple: Sometimes corrupt local officials ignore central-government directives. President Hu Jintao has said official corruption is a pervasive problem that the central government must tackle. The state-owned newspapers *China Daily* and *Global Times* reported that 4,000 corrupt officials have smuggled $50 billion in state funds out of the country over the last 30 years. Hu has made cracking down on corruption a major tenet of his administration. Under Hu, anticorruption police arrested Communist Party of China Shanghai Committee Secretary Chen Liangyu and sentenced him to 18 years in prison, on charges of financial fraud, abuse of power, and accepting bribes. The former vice mayors of bustling coastal cities Hangzhou and Suzhou were executed for taking millions in bribes. Despite attempts by the central government to eradicate corruption, it remains a serious problem—especially at the local level—that constantly undermines the Beijing authorities.

Local official corruption is a large reason why the food sector has been disrupted by poor quality despite the best intentions of the central government. Local officials are paid poorly, many earning only a few hundred dollars a month—less than the workers stapling furniture together in Laura Furniture's factories. They are not even allowed to travel abroad when they reach a certain rank, unless they are on officially sanctioned tours. Even powerful ministry heads make less than $2,000 a month. By comparison, most U.S. Cabinet secretaries make around $200,000 a year (or over $16,000 a month), and the average salary in the U.S. Department of Energy is over $5,000 a month.

Furthermore, the government restricts officials above a certain rank from transitioning into the private sector after they retire, so there are few avenues for local officials to make personal money aside from two sources: bribes, and relying on their children to earn for them. Retirement housing and food allowances for officials are contingent upon their continued support for the Communist Party, which makes their allegiance much easier to secure. The Party's control over housing benefits is a canny strategy aimed at discouraging divisive factions from emerging—it's hard to make trouble without an independent supply of cash and food. It is even rumored that all-powerful former Prime Ministers Li Peng and Zhu Rongji have been prevented from publishing memoirs. These restrictions and contingencies show the importance the Party places on ensuring harmony and limiting the power of one individual to disturb society.

Rules that limit officials' job hopping from the public to the private sector also ensure that decisions are in the country's best interests rather than for their personal future financial gains. Recall American officials such as former Secretary of the Treasury Robert Rubin or Vice President Dick Cheney, who ended up managing or lobbying for the industries or companies like Citigroup and Halliburton that they previously oversaw during their time in government. Sometimes I wonder if the decisions they made in office would have been different if they were barred from entering the private sector afterward.

Although these measures are designed to rein in corruption and ensure more objectivity among local officials, the result is that financial prospects for local officials are less impressive than for their Western counterparts or Chinese in the private sector. As in every country, some greedy local officials turn to corruption to enjoy a better life. They protect brothels out of simple greed, or to provide the best for their families, while they are still in office and have influence.

Many local officials also have no interest in getting promoted in the party hierarchy. They mainly care about how much leeway their direct supervisor grants them, rather than what the central government wants. As long as they don't threaten the primacy of the Party and thus threaten stability, they are given some flexibility in implementing state directives.

Corrupt officials protect illegal operations such as brothels as long as they do not cause spillover effects that harm their district, such as violence, forced prostitution, or drug use. They know that these will cause local citizens to protest, and that the central government will step in when that happens, so they seek to control them. Moreover, due to the large numbers of urban migrant workers, who are kept away from loved ones and family for months at a time, local officials understand that pragmatism must sometimes prevail over ideology or morality. They often turn a blind eye to prostitution so that male migrant workers are satisfied. One municipal official I spoke to saw it in practical terms, and summed the situation up this way: "Better they go to prostitutes than vent in other ways, like rape or causing social disorder."

For ordinary Chinese people, vices like drugs and violence are intolerable due to the immediate impact on their everyday lives, but often they will tolerate prostitution as long as it is kept behind closed doors and distant. Here we see the divide in thinking between levels of government: Local officials and people confront prostitution pragmatically, whereas the central government upholds a more morality-based approach.

On the other hand, restrictions on televised portrayals of sex and and campaigns against Internet pornography are run by ministries that report directly to the central government in Beijing. Unlike corrupt local officials, who expect to remain in their current positions, those who report to the higher administration in Beijing enforce national directives to the letter, because they aspire to rise within the Party hierarchy. This is why you end up with professors in Nanjing being arrested for arranging sex parties (under "licentiousness" statutes), while hookers ply their trade in pink-lit barber shops in front of policemen patrolling the streets. The orgy-organizing professor was arrested because he was using the Internet to arrange his trysts. This made it impossible for him to bribe someone for protection, because the ministries overseeing the Internet report directly to leaders in Beijing.

The conflict between official policies on prostitution and pornography versus their actual implementation at the local level symbolizes the many divergent interests between regional and central governments. Despite the central government's power to set national directives, it is not quite the monolithic and totalitarian state that many Westerners imagine. My friend Jack discovered this complexity via the pink brothels glittering along the ⁓⁓⁓⁓ ⁓⁓⁓⁓ ⁓⁓⁓⁓ ⁓⁓ ⁓⁓⁓ ⁓⁓⁓⁓ ⁓⁓ ⁓⁓⁓ ⁓⁓⁓ ⁓⁓⁓⁓⁓ ⁓⁓⁓ dichotomy, but ordinary Chinese people walk along these streets and live within this system. Their understanding of this duality explains why they often direct their anger at local governments, accusing them of corruption, while remaining generally supportive of the central government, which they trust to have the interests of the general public in mind.

When high-level officials are found guilty of corruption, they often receive serious punishments that help mollify some of the anger. Zheng Xiaoyu, the former director of the State Food and Drug Association, was executed for corruption in 2007. The former railway minister, Liu Zhijun, has been arrested for allegedly stealing over $100 million. He is being blamed for cutting corners on safety, which may have helped cause the July 24, 2011, train crash that killed 39 people and injured hundreds. He most likely will face a similar fate to Zheng's.

In China, competing interests, local and regional officials, and various government ministries are often given room to diverge from the central administration. This is actually a healthy situation, since it forces the central government to listen to other voices that are closer to the common people and to form a consensus among different orders in society to develop a unified strategy going forward.

One of the biggest problems facing China today is forced land appropriations and the eviction of peasants, done to allow real estate developers to build more housing units or so the government can launch new infrastructure projects like high-speed railways or subway systems. Many unsavory local officials, bribed by real estate developers, use corrupt local police and thugs to drive peasants out of their homes to build new projects. Because local governments often raise the bulk of their tax revenue from land sales, or their officials benefit from family relationships, some of them push for real estate development at all costs. They often do not adequately compensate those that need to be relocated. The more courageous citizens fight back against this injustice. In some instances, thugs are sent to beat and maim holdouts, and riots spill out into the general population.

Fueled by bubbling anger at endemic local corruption, these riots soon turn into massive conflagrations. Thousands of people quickly congregate and start causing bedlam. Protesters generally are not trying to overthrow the entire political system, but just attempting to stop what they see as thievery and brutish behavior on the part of local officials.

Western analysts often wrongly blame the central government for these battles, or assume that rioting means that local populations want to overthrow the government, similar to what happened in Egypt and Tunisia during the Arab Spring. International news media often gloss over the distinction between local and central governments or miss it entirely, so many times mass protests against corrupt local authorities in small, county-level cities get framed in the headlines as demonstrations against "Beijing" or "the Chinese government" that threaten their very legitimacy.

However, the central government does not condone these practices. The state-run *China Daily*, for instance, quoted research results from the Centre for Research on Social Contradictions that showed the biggest cause for unrest and mass protest in 2010 was forced evictions. They point to unfair local officials as the cause for nearly 180,000 instances of mass protest in that year. Prime Minister Wen Jiabao has also issued edicts preventing local police from participating in forced evictions and demolitions. Central authorities have also banned the use of violence and coercion to force people to move, and have pushed for giving evicted homeowners the right to appeal.

Yet with the money and skullduggery involved with real estate (*The Hurun Report* found that 23.5 percent of the 1,000 wealthiest Chinese earned their money primarily through real estate development), the situation is bound to worsen if the government does not enforce regulations in place.

The anger is very real, and for people who lost their homes, anger can potentially erupt into violence. Most people I have spoken to who have been evicted against their will are enraged, but believe the blame rests squarely on corrupt local officials in bed with real estate developers, rather than the whole government system.

Beijing's leaders understand the direness of the situation. One senior leader exasperatedly told me, "We have to stop these thugs at the local level. Some of these people are truly evil. Some of these people act like gods and are not intent on helping the people, but enriching themselves. They don't care about anyone but themselves." One of the problems that has prevented crackdowns is the difficulty of controlling local officials, especially if they have powerful patrons at the central-government level.

Many officials fear that the rot is far too widespread to be able to crack down easily, so they arrest a few high-profile people in the hopes of scaring the rest into order.

Local officials are given an extent of freedom that allows them to adjust application of policies to the local situation. However, the central government feels it needs to maintain its grip on power over local governments whenever it can, as well as the whole country, precisely because rampant corruption at the local level disrupts social stability and hurts everyday citizens. Central-government officials think that if they let their control slip and delegate their power, chaos could ensue. They are wary of American-style direct elections for the same reason. One official I spoke to summed up the government's worries about elections this way: "Imagine how corrupt it would be if we had elections," he said. "All the corrupt real estate developers could beat people up and intimidate voters to get their man elected. It would only hurt the people. We cannot allow elections when local officials in cahoots with tycoons could intimidate voters."

One cool spring day in Shanghai, I got a firsthand taste of how many of these demonstrations must be developing in cities all over China. I was driving along a main thoroughfare near a Carrefour hypermarket, when suddenly dozens of balloons flew into the air. As they made their way into the gray sky above, my son Tom, sitting in the backseat, shouted and pleaded that he wanted one.

I turned to the place from where the balloons seemed to be ascending. As we got closer, I saw a dark-skinned man, wearing blackened clothes that looked more like rags, yelling at a parked van. Inside was a group of four *chengguan*—local officials from the City Urban Administrative and Law Enforcement Bureau, or city enforcers.

Most problems with government thuggishness are not due to the normal police—the *gongan,* officers from the public safety bureaus—but to the chengguan. They are poorly trained, lowest-level security enforcers, often people who had been unemployed. The government gives them jobs to help enforce routine laws, like clearing out unlicensed street vendors. As one vendor told me while hurriedly packing up her stock of mugs, "I'm not afraid of police; they are polite. It is them," she said, pointing at a group of chengguan. "They hit." They are not a part of the police force, but many Western journalists don't make the distinction when they publish reports about fights or protests in Chinese cities. In fact, in my experience, the Chinese police are for the most part quite well trained and responsive to the needs of the people.

I went up to the roadside balloon salesman, who was near tears. He told me that the chengguan approached him without warning. He said they took out a machete-like knife, told him that he was not allowed to sell balloons, and cut the strings on the balloons, sending them all spiraling into the sky. He told me he had lost two weeks' wages. I could see him wondering how he would pay for his family's food, so I gave him money to cover his losses and confronted the chengguan in the van.

A group of furious onlookers surrounded the van and started yelling at the chengguan. Some started taking videos of the scene on their mobile phones. They had all seen what had happened. People started shouting that it was not right for the chengguan to simply take the balloon salesman's livelihood away, especially when so many officials are corrupt. One man yelled that if the man had paid a bribe, he would have been allowed to keep his balloons.

Tensions ran high outside the van as the screaming continued. Inside the van, the four chengguan looked bored and ignored us. After about five minutes, the chengguan in the driver's seat turned the ignition. Everyone outside parted and the van just drove off. And that was that—everyone just dispersed.

This situation probably would count as a situation of unrest, one that gets tabulated by the government among the hundreds of thousands of yearly instances of social instability, and which Western analysts use to indicate growing dissatisfaction with the government—but that would be an exaggeration.

Certainly no one in the crowd wanted to overthrow the central government and the entire administrative system. They, like me, simply wanted more accountability from the chengguan. In fact, many people in the crowd I spoke with said they wished the central government would do a better job of educating the chengguan. A middle-aged man who joined the crowd told me, "It is tough. Those chengguan are probably just are doing what they are told to do. None of us like it. They need jobs too. I hope the government can train them better."

Often, local officials simply ignore central-government regulations meant to protect everyday people, which explains why Chinese can support the central government while still protesting brutishness at the local level. Aside from this contention, there is also much debate in different parts of the government over the best policies for the country. For some reason, Western media often oversimplify the political legislative process in China. They perpetuate the inaccurate notion that all decisions originate from the nine old men on the Politburo Standing Committee, completely insulated from external opinion or input. Western media portray these nine men as only caring about how to enrich themselves and their families, while perpetuating their own power through fear and violence.

The reality is that the Standing Committee of the Politburo does not exist within a vacuum. Members, like leaders in the democratic countries, also have constituents that they need to represent and placate. In many ways, because of the lack of direct elections, they have to listen to the needs to their constituents even more closely than members of elected governments. After all, in the West, voting only displaces people, but transitions in Communist countries are far rockier.

If we analyze one of the hottest topics in policy circles around the world right now, the exchange rate of the renminbi and its race with the U.S. dollar, it is obvious that senior leaders are not making decisions in a bubble, but are in fact listening and getting pressured by different constituencies. How the debate plays out within China will help senior officials make this key monetary decision, in an example of bottom-up-generated policy.

Many economists like Nobel Prize winner and *New York Times* columnist Paul Krugman argue that China artificially manipulates its currency to keep it low compared to the U.S. dollar to ensure that China's exports remain cheaper. With the renminbi artificially low, Krugman argues, American manufacturers outsource to Chinese factories rather than to those in the United States. Krugman calls China a "bad actor" for its policies, and in a column titled "The Chinese Disconnect," he says it is "stealing" American jobs by running a "beggar thy neighbor" currency strategy that undermines global growth.

Even though the Chinese government has allowed the renminbi to appreciate over 25 percent in the last five years, Krugman argues that the Chinese government is stealing jobs from hardworking American citizens. However, as the Laura

Furniture case in Chapter 2 showed, it is far more likely that American firms would relocate factories from China to Vietnam or Indonesia, or keep manufacturing in China and simply increase end prices to the American consumer. It is unlikely that companies across most industries will shift production back to America.

Hu Jintao has repeatedly stated that the Chinese government will raise the renminbi, but at a slow and steady pace, to ensure stability in world financial markets and allow for long-term business planning. The renminbi has appreciated against the U.S. dollar by more than 25 percent since de-pegging from the dollar in 2005. Disregarding for a moment the economic reasons why the renminbi should or should not appreciate, let's take a look at the different constituencies within China that influence Hu and other senior officials' plan of overseeing a gradual appreciation rather than a faster revaluation.

The first constituency is manufacturers and their employees. Domestic factory owners making low-value goods like toys in places like Guangdong Province often operate on paper-thin margins of 2 to 3 percent. Their margins are getting squeezed further by soaring labor and real estate costs, leaving thousands of them at the cusp of bankruptcy. These factories employ tens of thousands of workers, are often connected to local officials through family relationships, and supply local government coffers with tax revenue.

For this group, a strong renminbi would further accelerate factory shutdowns already being precipitated by rising costs. For this reason, the manufacturing constituency has been lobbying hard to delay increases in the value of the renminbi. They want to slow the outward flow of Western brands, such as Laura Furniture, that are relocating manufacturing or sourcing operations to lower-cost markets like Indonesia or Vietnam.

In 2010 I met with Mr. Xu, a clothing accessories factory owner from the southeastern coastal city Wenzhou, for an interview. Mr. Xu grew up dirt poor in Zhejiang Province in the 1970s. He told me getting access to food was a daily challenge for his family. Through years of hard work, he has built up a clothing accessory empire, and is now one of China's one million U.S.-dollar millionaires. He has a Mercedes and a BMW, and owns luxurious homes in different cities in China—and even several in Italy. We were sitting in one of his homes in Shanghai, a palatial apartment with breathtaking view overlooking the Huangpu River.

An appreciating renminbi lulls my margins. I do not want it," Mr. Xu told me. "It will mean that I have to shut my factories down." Nearly every one of the dozens of factory executives I have spoken has echoed this exact sentiment. Mr. Xu's operations were big enough to make him rich, but they were not big enough for him to be able to relocate to other markets or regions, so he was facing factory closures.

Local governments in factory-laden municipalities have been lobbying the central government alongside factory owners against a fast-appreciating renminbi. Shuttering factories would hurt these regions' tax revenue, cause massive unemployment, and potentially spur destabilizing labor unrest. There is a more important and much more personal reason local officials are equally anxious: namely, that GDP growth is one of the major criteria upon which they are judged to determine future promotion potential.

On the other hand, other factions and constituencies are lobbying for an appreciation of the renminbi. Energy companies that have to buy oil priced in U.S. dollars on the open market, for instance, would benefit. The government caps end prices of energy and gasoline for consumers in order to ward off civil unrest and inflation. Oil and energy prices have gone up in China over the last several years, but far slower than the rise of oil prices in the international markets, which is eroding energy firms' margins.

Brownouts occurred in the summer of 2011 in 10 major manufacturing provinces because energy companies cut back on power generation. Former Prime Minister Li Peng's daughter, Li Xiaolin, who runs China Power International Development, one of China's largest energy companies, has pointed out that energy companies' problems are due to rising commodity costs.

There are also groups that want the renminbi to appreciate even faster than energy firms do. Factions within the government that want to lower China's trade surplus with America and other nations, and to move China away from high-pollution manufacturing toward more sustainable service businesses, are pushing for higher consumption. They urge greater appreciation of the renminbi to allow everyday Chinese to buy more goods.

Groups urging a stronger renminbi are motivated by the fear that China will fall into the "middle income trap," as many developing countries, like Mexico, have done. The trap is a per capita GDP of about $6,000, at which point it is common for average salaries to stagnate, while the gap between the wealthy and the poor increases. To avoid the income gap and becoming a failed developing economy, Zhou Xiaochuan, the governor of the People's Bank of China (the country's central bank), has made it a priority to try and implement better social security and medical benefits, so that everyday Chinese feel more confident about their future well-being and are willing to spend more. Zhou has made it clear that stimulating more consumption will be a key goal of the central bank in the coming years.

Government institutions also support a faster appreciation of the renminbi. Some officials in the Ministry of Health are worried that pollution is causing the state-run medical system to creak under the pressure. They have told me they also want the renminbi to appreciate, which they believe will accelerate the shutdown of high-polluting factories, whose emissions are a major source of public health problems such as higher cancer rates. For these officials, who see their hospital budgets getting hit hard by pollution-related diseases, weaning the country away from low-value manufacturing to a more domestic-consumption and service-oriented market would be critical; the appreciation of the renminbi would help this cause.

Manufacturers, energy companies, central bankers, health officials—these are just some of the various constituencies that are lobbying for and against renminbi appreciation and vying to influence China's future currency policies. In the midst of all these sometimes conflicting interests sit the central-government decision makers. The central government must consider all of these important constituencies while thinking strategically about where to steer the country overall. It needs to ensure that the country moves toward a sustainable growth model without alienating powerful interest groups and destroying short-term economic growth. It is an extremely delicate balance to strike.

As noted, the Chinese central government has more people to satisfy than in a democratically elected administration, because its legitimacy derives from the satisfaction of different constituencies with its policies, rather than just one particular side or base. The central government needs to throw bones to and mollify many diverse sectors, because it does not have the numerical legitimacy that an open, democratic vote would provide. It is within this complicated matrix that its policies are conceived and decided upon.

One benefit of this model of governance is that all constituencies understand that they will have to compromise to be part of the consensus. This understanding minimizes risks of overt factionalism that could lead to a return to the chaos and radicalism within leadership circles that I highlighted in Chapter 3. Compromise and leading by consensus have been the hallmarks of leadership under President Hu Jintao, which contrasts greatly with the grandstanding and total lack of compromise in the U.S. Congress during the debt-ceiling crisis, during which Standard & Poor downgraded America's debt precisely because of the inability of its political leaders to compromise and do what was best for the country and the world economy.

CASE STUDIES
WHAT TO DO AND WHAT NOT TO DO IN CHINA

- Do Not Assume the Chinese Government Is Monolithic

    China's government is not one large bureaucracy. Different ministries and levels of government (central, provincial, and municipal) often have divergent and competing interests. Gaining support and approval from all levels remains critical; otherwise, companies might face fines, delays, and even outright asset seizures.

    BYD, an electric car company in which Warren Buffet has invested, forgot this simple rule when it started factory construction in Xiamen on plots zoned for agricultural land. Construction started after local authorities approved the project, but BYD had failed to get central-government approval. It seized BYD's land and factory for over a year until the land was rezoned for industrial use.

    Before starting construction, BYD should have won approval from both the local and central governments. This approval process is especially important for larger projects that are water

---

and resource intensive and heavily polluting—both key areas of concern for the central government. One chemical company told me they were denied the licenses to build a $1 billion chemical plant at the height of the financial crisis, despite huge support from the provincial government, because of fears over the resulting pollution and water use. A senior official told me it would be impossible to get approval for a project of this size, given its potential level of pollution.

China is no longer like the Wild West, where local officials can green-light projects at odds with key central-government directives like reducing pollution. Eventually the central government will clamp down to ensure compliance with national directives.

Key Action Item

Never launch big initiatives with the support of the local government but not the central one. The central government's wishes will ultimately prevail, no matter how many connections local interests have. The business landscape is littered with ventures that failed because support was not gained from enough layers of the government.

• Understand Chinese Officials Are People, Too

Many Western executives seem to think of some Chinese officials as evil, corrupt, two-faced Party apparatchiks. Others are seen as spineless hacks keeping their heads down. Do not forget they have the same self-motivations all people have—they want to be able to care for their families, get promoted, and stay out of trouble.

Getting approval for groundbreaking projects is difficult not because frontline officials lack imagination or are corrupt, but because they do not want their careers derailed if something goes wrong with the project. It is easier and safer to keep one's head down.

One American private-equity firm chairman told me he was frustrated he could not get permission to invest in a heart-disease hospital. It did not make sense, he told me, as he had money and a top-10 university hospital from America lined up as his partner. Demand by wealthy Chinese for private cardiology services was soaring, and expatriates also might want a heart-disease clinic that met international standards. Despite spending millions in up-front investment costs and years preparing the venture, the problem was that he simply could not get approval from local Ministry of Health officials. He assumed they wanted bribes or were unqualified.

As I spoke with local officials, it was clear they were worried about green-lighting the project unless someone from way up top in Beijing publicly agreed with the project. For something like heart surgery and wealthy Chinese as the clients, the risks to their careers outweighed the benefits. Death was common, and so were the odds of a messy public fight with well-connected Chinese. They decided it was better to delay approval on the project until someone with more political capital came along. In the meantime, it was easier to approve projects like dental clinics that held much less risk.

Key Action Item

When navigating China's bureaucracy, understand the needs and motivations of local officials. Many want to green-light projects to get more tax revenue, but fear drawing negative attention to themselves. Garnering support from local officials for trailblazing projects is key, but so is getting the patronage of someone higher up who is either willing to take risks or has so much political capital that one errant project won't harm his career.

- Do Not Overestimate the Importance of *Guanxi*

    Foreign executives often hear the term *guanxi* and assign almost mystical importance to the concept. They define guanxi as "connections," and many are told that good guanxi gives you everything—without it, it is impossible to do anything in China.

Rather than defining guanxi as "connections," "circle of trust" is a more apt definition. Like most developing countries, China operates in a low-trust environment, so it is critical to do business with people within your circle of trust so that you won't get cheated or have problems in timing, accounts receivable, or quality control.

It is almost impossible for foreigners to gain true guanxi in China unless they have lived there for a long time (10 years or more at a minimum), were schoolmates with younger Chinese, or married a local Chinese person and were brought into her circle of trust. Most Chinese view foreigners as only being around for the short term, so the feeling is that they should try to profit from them as much as possible right away.

Much of the true guanxi has been forged through familial networks or by being neighbors at the village level for generations, which is something most foreigners posted in China for a few years can never realistically hope to achieve.

It is important to build relationships in China, much as it is anywhere in the world—perhaps even a little more so, because of the low-trust environment. But executives should never fool themselves by overestimating the importance of guanxi. They should also never base an entire project on guanxi, because when the winds of power shift, they may be left in trouble.

Connections can be a double-edged sword. They will not get you everything, but they can cost you everything. Take Zhang Rongkun, who was a close business connection of Shanghai's former Communist Party Chief, Chen Liangyu. When Chen was toppled, so was Rong, and he was sentenced to decades behind bars. Whenever a key government official is arrested, so are the business leaders surrounding him, and the government often gives businessmen tougher sentences than officials.

When new officials take over from old ones, especially if their power was won in a factional fight, they will often cut out or make life difficult for businessmen too closely aligned with their predecessors. It is far better to have strong, close relations with leadership in general, than to be seen as too close to any specific official or faction.

Key Action Item

While it is important for foreigners to build trust with partners, never forget that most Chinese will always view you as a foreigner who will only be there for the short term. Always be wary of people who say they can essentially sell you their guanxi; it's probably no good, because people do not easily share their guanxi. As China continues to adhere to more international business practices, what you know will become as important as who you know.

7

CHINA'S REAL ESTATE SECTOR

BOOM OR BUST OR SOMETHING ELSE?

The fumes were like nothing I have ever experienced. My stomach churned, my head pounded, and I was scared I was going to faint or die from the odor. I finished up my duties as fast as I could and ran out, covering my mouth and nose.

I was not walking the floor of a chemical plant inhaling toxic waste, but in the bathroom of my friends' home. Nearly a decade and a half later, my nose still burns and my eyebrows twitch when I think of the revolting smell wafting from that bathroom.

My friends Winnie and Karen were young twentysomethings when they invited me to their home to spend the night and to see how everyday urban Chinese lived in the late 1990s. I was so excited because at that time, Chinese did not invite many foreigners over for a visit—let alone overnight—probably out of fear of neighbors talking, or embarrassment from being too poor.

Until then I had visited maybe a dozen homes, but I had never slept over at one. Most of the people I had visited were professors or government officials. It always seemed they had approval to invite me over. Even officials' homes were insanely tiny and cramped, more like walk-in closets than homes, really. The rooms were dark, and every last piece of space up to the ceiling was filled with boxes. Despite being cramped, the homes I had visited thus far belonged to the elite classes; I wanted to see how most urban Chinese lived, in the ramshackle buildings that dotted the landscape.

Winnie and Karen were everyday Chinese people, working as clerks selling socks in a state-owned department store in Tianjin. I had met them one night a few weeks earlier in one of the few dancing halls in town, Kung Hao, a massive, 1,500-person-capacity club that was full of partygoers seven days a week. People would buy tickets and start dancing in the afternoon, take a break for dinner, and then come back in the evening to maximize the value of their ticket. I had become famous there as one of the few foreigners who regularly attended. The manager had even asked me to dance for a while in one of the cages above the crowd, and I became an attraction—I'm not sure if it was because I was a good dancer or that I was a subject of curiosity—until the military owners disliked the spectacle and ordered me down.

I had become friends with Winnie and Karen after meeting on the dance floor. Staying with them would let me see how everyday Chinese lived—and was when I first started to see the subhuman conditions in which most Chinese then lived, and unfortunately in which many still do.

When I first arrived at Winnie and Karen's home, the block housing where they lived looked like it could collapse at any time. The façade was covered in giant cracks and blackened by mold and soot. Then–Prime Minister Zhu Rongji railed against poorly constructed buildings and launched campaigns to clamp down on construction that allowed for unsafe structures. He called tottering buildings "tofu construction" because they looked solid but were really weak and cracked or collapsed easily. Prime Minister Zhu's warnings would be prescient a decade later, after the tragic 2008 Sichuan earthquake, when too many buildings collapsed and shoddy school construction caused students to die.

The entranceway to the crumbling, tofu-like building was completely black, and I bumped into bicycles strewn about as I walked in. As with many Chinese apartment buildings, to save money and electricity the stairways were dark except for solitary, motion-sensitive bulbs on landings that flickered dimly when activated.

When the light finally flickered to life, I saw rusted pipes dangling from the ceiling, seemingly ready to drop but held up miraculously by thin pieces of wire and rope. Exposed wires coiled and twisted around in the corner. As Winnie and I made our way up the stairwell to their eighth-floor apartment, paint and putty sloughed off the walls.

Waiting for us at the top of the landing, Karen opened the door with a beaming smile and welcomed me in. Their home was one of the smallest I had ever seen. It seemed to be no larger than the back of a Ford pickup truck. Winnie and Karen had squeezed two toddler-sized beds together, which also served as their sitting and eating area. There was no mattress, only hard wooden planks and a grubby sheet as a blanket. As the guest, they told me I would sleep on the wood-mattress bed, which had a pillow stained with years of head grease and sweat. Just looking at the pillow made my hair itch.

As we sat down and started to talk, Karen said, "I know this apartment might seem small and dirty compared to wealthy Westerners, but this is better than what we get in the countryside. Back at home, we have dirt floors and no running water. We have to pump the water ourselves from a well that we share with several families. Our home is also better than the dormitory-style accommodation many companies offer employees, where eight people share a room with bunk beds stacked to the ceiling."

Over the next few years, I visited more homes and dormitories and found the condition of Karen and Winnie's home was fairly common for far too many everyday urban Chinese. Many lived scrunched together in impossibly tiny homes that often stank or seemed ready to collapse. I would define the accommodations that many of these homes offer as subhuman—barely fit for farm animals. Migrant workers in Beijing have moved into desolate underground tunnels built as fallout shelters decades ago. Stories abound of migrant workers living in public bathrooms because there is running water and light.

The lack of affordable, decent-quality housing is one of the biggest problems facing China today. Soaring home prices and substandard living conditions for too many people cause depression and anger among lower-income classes that could threaten social stability if not adequately addressed. One common joke among construction workers, who use their hands and sweat to put up towering apartment blocks, is that it will take them one year of labor to be able to buy one square meter of the apartment they just built—or a decade to buy the toilet area.

One of the main goals of the five-year plan the central government announced for 2011 was to address the common complaint that decent housing is too expensive by building more affordable homes and rental units for poor Chinese. The government announced that it will construct 10 million units of affordable housing, but even that will not be enough. Having decent housing that won't collapse under heavy storms is a human rights issue.

One major global debate is whether or not there has been too much housing and infrastructure construction in China. Many economists estimate nearly 50 percent of the country's economy deals directly with real estate, and local governments derive much of their tax base from land sales because few cities have any kind of annual property tax in place. This has caused a dangerous cycle, in which local governments push land sales to get tax revenue for short-term spending while creating unsustainable long-term real estate developments. Because of restrictions on issuing municipal bonds, some local governments establish real estate companies and compel local branches of state-owned banks to lend them money, just to pump liquidity into the system. Fears that the numbers of nonperforming loans made for poorly crafted real estate projects will rise are hitting the financial sector, and the central government's Huijin sovereign fund has had to buy shares to prop values up.

If China's real estate sector collapses, the reasoning goes, the subsequent financial collapse would spur a domino effect that could take down the world economy worse than what followed the 2008 Lehman Brothers collapse. Global demand for iron ore and other commodities used in construction that have fueled booms in Australia and Canada would drop, sending those nations' economies into a tailspin in an already-fragile world economy. Banks with exposure would fail and need to be bailed out.

Many analysts, like famed hedge fund manager and short seller Jim Chanos—who proudly states that he has never been to China—have made waves in financial circles by questioning whether there is enough demand for all the homes being built, and whether too much leverage is being taken out by home buyers. Chanos thinks China's real estate market is on a "treadmill to hell" and will collapse far harder than Dubai's. Other economists, like New York University professor Nouriel "Dr. Doom" Roubini, argue that China's infrastructure spending on railroads, airports, and highways has been wasteful in triplicate. Roubini predicts that China will suffer a serious slowdown sometime in 2013 due to inefficient and wasteful construction.

At first glance, Roubini's and Chanos's fears seem to have merit. Housing prices throughout the country have soared since the late 1990s, when the government started to allow people to buy homes for the first time. Twenty percent annual increases in housing prices have been typical throughout the country, even after the government implemented strict mortgage controls in 2010. Overall, housing prices more than tripled between 2005 and 2009 and have risen faster than average wages. The average price per square meter in Shanghai is over $3,500.

Row upon row of empty apartment buildings dot the landscape, despite the demand for housing by people like Winnie and Karen. There are even ghost cities like Erdos, an entire city built for one million residents that lies empty.

Infrastructure spending has also driven major economic growth. New tunnels and bridges seem to emerge overnight, and many question how safe such rapid construction can be—especially in light of the 2011 high-speed train crash that killed dozens and injured hundreds—and whether it is even needed. Much of China's four-trillion-renminbi stimulus program, launched in 2008 to combat the Great Recession, went toward enlarging and expanding current infrastructure projects. Government plans to spend $300 billion on high-speed rail to carry passengers and cargo to every part of the country are now being reconsidered due to safety concerns. Still, over 6,000 miles of rail have already been opened, and another 11,000 miles are under construction and set to open by 2015. Nearly one million Chinese continue to take high-speed trains every day.

Subway construction to reduce congestion in cities has also been a major initiative. Shanghai alone has laid down more subway lines than there are in New York City. Beijing has opened 209 miles of subway track and 174 stations for its 14 lines. It has plans to spend $90 billion to extend the track by over 220 miles by 2020. Traffic has gotten so bad in Beijing that the capital city limits what days some cars can drive, because it can take hours to go just a few miles.

As of 2011, over three dozen cities have submitted plans to the central government to construct subway lines. Even with all the new subway construction, taking a train during rush hour can be a harrowing experience because the subway cars get packed. In my decade of regularly riding subways here, I can probably count on one hand the number of times I have secured a seat.

Airports have also seen tremendous growth. Shanghai's Pudong International Airport has been expanding to keep pace with traffic by opening new terminals and runways. Passenger traffic grew 27 percent in 2010, to 40.6 million passengers. Pudong Airport is now the third-busiest airport in the world in terms of freight traffic, with 3,227,914 metric tons handled every year.

The fast growth and high prices would make it seem that there has been too much infrastructure and real estate spending, and give credence to Roubini and Chanos's arguments.

However, both of them overestimate the amount of leverage involved in these projects. They also use phantom facts in deriving their conclusions (for instance, Roubini has criticized Shanghai for opening new airports when it has not done so since 1999, and said that a maglev train connects Shanghai to Hangzhou when, in fact, there is not one) and underestimate the demand for cheaper housing and greater business efficiency.

The need for less-expensive housing and commercial space will require urban areas to spread out, and for all infrastructure spending to be used on railroads, subways, and airports. Aside from the terrible living conditions in which too many Chinese live due to overcrowding and lack of affordable housing, companies are having big problems finding good location for a store or office. Traffic also makes it difficult to arrange face-to-face business meetings. A shortage of retail spaces that can accommodate the needs of foreign retailers wishing to expand their outlets has also increased the demand for more infrastructure spending.

One executive of a large French home-decoration retailer told me, "We have plans to open fifty stores in the next three years, but one of the major limiting factors is finding locations that are affordable. Rents are sky high and vacancies hard to find." Commercial rents along Shanghai's famed Nanjing Road shopping district are now the 29th most expensive in the world, when you can even get a spot. Cities need better transportation infrastructure to reduce costs and congestion, allow for more efficient business, and attract investment dollars.

If rising labor costs are the first major trend spurring the End of Cheap China, soaring real estate prices are the second, increasing costs for businesses and making profits harder to squeeze out of the country.

Many economists focus on monetary supply, and average wages relative to total land prices, to determine whether the real estate market is healthy or not. Largely forgotten in this debate are the subhuman conditions in which most Chinese live today. More housing and infrastructure spending are needed just to create basic living conditions that people can afford. The expansion of cities will create more business opportunities, which will allow incomes to rise further. A two-minute walk in any direction from the heart of Shanghai's financial district will find millions living in subpar conditions. To ensure stability, the government must advocate and support more affordable housing at any cost.

Even for middle-class Chinese families, it is typical for three generations to live in 300 square foot apartments in towering high rises with few green areas. Buildings are squeezed together and remind me of sardines when I look down at them from airplanes. In comparison, the average house in America is 2,330 square feet, according to the National Association of Home Builders. That doesn't even include lawns and terraces, which are common in America but are luxuries reserved for only the superrich in China.

Most Chinese restaurant and construction workers live in dormitories provided by their employers and often board eight people to a room. Think of pictures you've seen of overcrowding in California jails, then double the nastiness factor. California jails are cleaner and probably built of sturdier and less toxic materials.

Simply from a human-rights standpoint, there is a clear demand for more and better housing. The government doesn't want to have slums and shantytowns pop up, as in America and the Philippines. Overleveraging in the residential sector is not really the problem Chanos believes it to be, either, as for years the government has been limiting the amount of debt one can take out when buying homes to prevent the market from overheating. In cities like Shanghai, home buyers must put 30 percent down for their first home and 50 percent for their second; they cannot buy a third home anymore. Speculation has not hit China as it did in the United States, where people earning $25,000 dollars a year could put zero percent down and buy multiple properties. Even if housing prices were to fall 20 percent or more, panic selling would not occur as it did in the United States or Dubai, because few house buyers have much debt and their mortgages would not be underwater.

The major problem in the real estate industry is not whether there is too much empty housing or too much debt in the residential sector, but whether everyday Chinese will ever be able to afford buying the available homes, and if enough low-income housing will be built. The average Shanghai resident will have to work 50 years at current per capita earning rates to buy a decent home, versus 10 years for a U.S. resident.

Most developers have focused on building more lucrative luxury apartments to earn fatter profit margins and to satisfy the demand of the moneyed class, whose earnings have been rising far faster than average Chinese wages. These blocks often rise up in the middle of poorer areas, raising tensions and increasing dissatisfaction.

Because of the severe limit on the number of homes one can buy now and on who can buy them, there is a massive, pent-up demand for housing. Many home buyers are sitting on the sidelines, expecting prices to soften. Other would-be home buyers who don't qualify to buy homes now are waiting to do so once restrictions ease.

One serious problem emerging in the real estate sector is there has been far too much construction on the commercial side, where regulations that limit building on credit have been less pronounced. In the first half of 2011, my firm interviewed dozens of real estate developers. The vast majority of residential property developers said they were going to switch and build more commercial projects, because it was easier for them to get credit from banks for those projects. Chinese real estate billionaire Zhang Xin, the chief executive officer of SOHO China Ltd., told the Shanghai Foreign Correspondents' Club in an August 2011 speech that all of SOHO's 11.4 billion renminbi of investment in Shanghai was on the commercial side in 2011, because government restrictions on residential development made office buildings a safer bet.

Many commercial projects are ill advised, however, and represent an area where the central government needs to increase its oversight. Many will likely fail, because developers often do not have the management and branding expertise to make their malls fit consumers' needs. Ultimately they will not be able to charge high rents or get revenue splits, and might not be able to pay off their debt. Too much investment in commercial real estate will also limit the amount of land available for home construction, which will also cause housing prices to rise too rapidly due to fixed supply. Overall, commercial projects only account for about 20 percent of real estate construction, so even a downturn there will not hurt the greater economy in a meaningful way, but it is an area where the government needs to watch closely.

While risks about a dangerous real estate bubble do exist, the benefits of massive construction far outweigh the risks, because reduced congestion will create a more affordable housing supply, make business interaction more efficient, and reduce pollution. It is also better to complete infrastructure projects now, when it is cheaper, because of soaring wage demands that will make it impossible in a decade to launch major infrastructure initiatives, as is currently the case in the United States.

Historically, countries like America and Japan spent huge proportions of their GDP on fixed investment, which was critical in preparing those nations for decades of economic growth. Investing in the national highway system under President Dwight D. Eisenhower in the 1950s provided the conditions necessary for efficient manufacturing and service sectors.

Considering how crowded urban areas in China are (Shanghai is the world's densest city, packing in 24 million people), the government absolutely needs to build more infrastructure projects. Critics like Carnegie Foundation Fellow and Guanghua School of Management professor Michael Pettis agree with Roubini. They both fret that the construction is inefficient and resembles building bridges to nowhere, as the Japanese did at the start of their financial problems in the 1990s. Also like Roubini, Pettis believes that China's infrastructure spending of about 50 percent accounts for too much of its overall GDP. However, there are huge differences between Chinese and Japanese construction for which Pettis fails to account.

China's railroads, bridges, and tunnels are increasing economic efficiency for the most part, not only within a city but between massive metropolitan areas. For instance, high-speed rail has cut travel time from 11 hours to 5 between Shanghai and Wuhan, increasing the business capabilities of the 40 million people who live in these cities. Not only is China's infrastructure spending more efficient than Japan's, it is helping to jumpstart economic growth. This is very different from Japan, where infrastructure investment was used to connect metropolitan areas to tiny hamlets, representing a desperate attempt to wake from its economic slumber after deflation (despite the low-interest loans made to pay for these projects) damaged the economy. The Japanese government continues to pour funding into these projects, while the residents of these small towns cannot make money on their own and need handouts to survive.

Japan's overall debt was 225.8 percent of GDP in 2010—the highest in the world, according to the International Monetary Fund—while China's is around 70 percent. Infrastructure spending in Japan continues largely to be wasteful, while in China it is setting the stage for economic growth.

My son Tom fell asleep for his afternoon nap one day when we were travelling on a bus to Ningbo, a seaport city of 2.2 million people to the south of Shanghai. We had just gotten on a bridge when he fell asleep. I had never been to Ningbo because it used to take five or more maddening hours stuck in traffic to get there.

When Tom woke up 30 minutes later, we were still on that bridge despite having driven at a good clip. A few minutes later, we arrived in Ningbo, three hours after we left Shanghai. The 27-kilometer-long bridge, the world's largest transoceanic bridge, opened in 2008 and cut travel time almost in half.

Since then, I have travelled to Ningbo repeatedly for business deals and vacation. Business efficiency is clearly being improved by construction projects like Ningbo's bridge. One of my clients in the food and beverage sector told me that because of increased logistical access to Ningbo, it would become a major investment area for his firm's outlets. He said, "Until the transportation system opened up, we were not really planning on opening retail outlets in Ningbo. The cost of business was too high. Now it is easy to ship product to Ningbo, and our senior managers can get there more easily, arriving from Shanghai in the morning and returning at night. Before it was a multiple-day trip, but now we expect to increase our investment in Ningbo."

New investment locations are opening up throughout the country, as in the case of my food and beverage client, precisely because of new infrastructure investment.

On the opposite side of the spectrum from Winnie and Karen's home are the homes of the truly rich. *The Hurun Report,* which has declared that China's billionaires might outnumber America's, has confirmed the identities of 271 of them, but they estimate at least another 200 Chinese have astronomical hidden wealth.

Wealth creation in China over the last decade has caused multimillion-dollar homes to proliferate. Contrary to the emerging conventional wisdom of some economists, however, these homes do not threaten financial stability. Government regulations require buyers of standalone villas to put down a 50 percent deposit and pay hefty transaction taxes if they are flipped in short periods of time. Strict rules supervising debt should eliminate fears that there is too much debt in the marketplace, but surprisingly many analysts do not acknowledge the lack of debt on the residential side of real estate.

I was zooming along in a billionaire's Ferrari on Beijing's streets when the owner, Mr. Chen, told me that he was now looking at buying a $15-million-plus home, because restrictions on the number of homes he could buy was forcing him to go more upmarket. Such restrictions on home acquisition were creating a new housing segment—homes ranging in the tens of millions of dollars—and helps explain why overall housing prices in China are continuing to rise, despite the weakening of mid-tier home prices and the collapse of sales volume after the government implemented strict mortgage rules in 2010 to permit a soft landing in the real estate sector.

Wealthy Chinese like Mr. Chen are seeing their incomes rise at a far faster pace than housing prices. Mr. Chen puts 100 percent down whenever he buys a home or auto. The number of U.S.-dollar billionaires doubled between 2010 and 2011, according to *Hurun,* and the number of millionaires is expected to grow to 2.4 million by 2013, up from 750,000 in 2009. Many of these wealthy Chinese are consolidating market share and boxing out competitors who cannot deal with the End of Cheap China. Their fortunes often rise by double or more every year.

My firm's research suggests that many of the wealthy prefer to buy real estate because it is a tangible asset; they do not trust equities due to accounting scandals. I was sitting in the enormous living room of Mr. Zhou, one of China's largest real estate developers, when he started to share his investing strategies and views on real estate with me. "I never buy Chinese stocks. Who can trust the accounting? It is far safer to buy real estate. There are too many Chinese without adequate housing, so demand will always outstrip supply." He continued, "There are no annual property taxes, so I just buy homes and leave them empty to resell at some point. At the end of the day, if things go wrong, you still have tangible assets if you buy property."

A cultural predilection for real estate, as well as fears over investing in other asset classes, also helps explain why the real estate sector continues to soar. With little end-buyer debt involved, worries of systemic risk are low. Cash-starved and overleveraged developers might collapse, and a consolidation in the industry (which favors larger and better connected players who have large credit lines) is likely, but this also signals a healthy maturation of the marketplace.

• • •

By contrast, the real estate sector in China is far from healthy. Far too many units sit empty, and far too many everyday Chinese do not have access to housing. Concerns about the safety and economic viability of many residential, commercial, and public infrastructure projects are legitimate.

One of the reasons for the ongoing safety problems actually stems from the weak financial system, which makes it difficult for entrepreneurs and small-business owners to tap credit. One real estate developer, Mr. Xu, told me that when he first started his business he had to accept a 75 percent interest rate over three months from an underground bank just to get enough capital to build a small building in southern China. The big state-owned banks laughed him out of their offices. Mr. Xu said he did whatever it took to earn a profit, and built a track record of managing large projects, so that he could get funding from the big banks.

Many smaller real estate developers like Mr. Xu construct buildings as fast as they can so they can sell them and pay back loans. They do not necessarily put up poor-quality buildings intentionally (although many do cut corners to squeeze out more profits), but many simply need to repay their debts. Being burdened by high loans and interest rates are minor concerns when taking loans from underground banks, which explains why so many Wenzhou entrepreneurs started fleeing creditors in the autumn of 2011.

Despite all of the problems in the real estate sector, the reality is that construction has to continue in order to provide adequate housing and improve business efficiency. The challenges that the economy will face if this does not happen—namely, social instability—are far worse than a potential downturn in housing prices. Debt problems have been greatly exaggerated, as have concerns about whether too much construction is taking place. The real issue involves execution and oversight to ensure the highest safety and efficiency. More of both are clearly needed.

CASE STUDIES
WHAT TO DO AND WHAT NOT TO DO IN CHINA

- A Good Location Is Hard to Get

Finding good locations for storefronts is difficult, as local governments redevelop entire sections of cities and push for massive building projects that end up being controlled by the larger real estate companies. Landlords often only sign deals with well-known brands, boxing out new brands or charging them astronomical rates. Other landlords are poor at mall management and offer unsuitable, disorganized retail spaces. Brands need to be patient and willing to grow slowly as they search for good locations at rents that allow them to generate a profit.

To combat the difficulty of finding these locations, some brands are becoming real estate developers themselves. Furniture retailer IKEA is building large mall complexes and has partnered with domestic electronics chain Suning and French supermarket retailer Auchan to be anchor tenants. This way, IKEA ensures good sites for its stores while it generates rental income.

Key Action Item

Brands are finding it increasingly difficult to find affordable, good locations. Companies might have to become landlords or follow more conservative growth plans.

- Look Beyond Beijing and Shanghai

Many Western brands such as Ralph Lauren look at the high average incomes in Shanghai and Beijing and decide to focus sales efforts there. But high real estate, labor, and advertising costs make it difficult to profit in first-tier cities. Ralph Lauren has made little headway in China because it has concentrated most of its retail outlet growth in expensive cities, when it should have expanded in fast-growing, second- or third-tier cities like Changsha with less competition and rising incomes.

Luxury apparel firm Ports Design has opened hundreds of points of sale while maintaining a small presence in Shanghai and Beijing. Few sales are made at these outlets because consumers demand the bigger mass-luxury names like Louis Vuitton and Gucci. In many lower-tier cities, however, where these brands have not yet begun to sell, Ports dominates the market.

Key Action Item

Companies should look beyond the well-worn path of Shanghai and Beijing to open shop where consumers have money and the demand for foreign products. There is less competition there, and consumers in those cities check to see if a brand has overseas outlets; they do not care about company presences in Shanghai and Beijing.

- Chinese Care About What Goes Inside Their Homes Now, Too

A decade ago, homes were so dirty and cramped that Chinese rarely brought guests home, because they were afraid of losing face. Most disposable income was spent on items people could see, such as cars, clothing, watches and jewelry, and mobile phones, to present an image of success to the outside world.

As Chinese got wealthier, they started to invite guests home but kept them in the living room. Wide-screen televisions became de rigueur, even in households of relatively modest wealth. The average wide-screen television sold in China is 42 inches, versus 37 inches in the United States.

Many analysts wrongly assume that Chinese simply do not care about making their homes nice. This is not true. Lack of spending is a function of poverty, rather than not wanting to spend money on home decoration.

As wealth in China increases, the trend is toward self-consumption and indulgence. One hot sector is bedding—products not shown to many outsiders. Surveys that my firm conducted in eight cities found expenditures on decorating bedrooms were rising faster than for any other room. Consumers buy wallpaper, furniture, small decorative items like vases, paintings, and bedding, which they use not to show status but to pamper themselves.

Key Action Item

Chinese consumer tastes are evolving as incomes rise. They no longer buy items only to show status, although this still plays a critical role in purchases of autos, clothing, footwear, and consumer electronics. Hot categories (e.g., bedding) are emerging, for which the motivations for purchase are not about status as much as comfort and self-fulfillment.

- In-Store Education and Individualism

   Consumers are often confused about how to use certain products. They worry about looking stupid and unsophisticated, so they often skip buying them. Companies can gain loyal customers by employing salespeople trained to educate consumers on how to use these products.

   For consumers who have not arrived at a store with a clear idea of what they wanted to buy, or did not know what to expect there, in-store displays and sales-staff expertise can be major motivating factors to buy specific brands and products.

   Wealthy people, peasants just a decade before, often go to luxury retailers like Zegna and order the entire set of clothes on a mannequin—shoes, socks, belt, pants, shirt, and cufflinks— because they are afraid of buying the wrong thing. They do not know how to mix and match clothing, and are very sensitive about being seen as lacking sophistication.

Key Action Item

Brands need to create informative in-store displays to help educate consumers on how to mix and use products, and should train staff how to educate consumers.

- Differentiate Your Product Selection in Retail Outlets, Because Most Chinese Won't Pay More for Service

Consumer electronics sales in China are soaring because Chinese want wide-screen televisions, air conditioners, and refrigerators. However, retailers like Best Buy have retreated from the market despite much fanfare about opening there. What went wrong for Best Buy?

Retailers like Best Buy cannot charge premiums for products when they sell the exact same items as local vendors. Chinese generally won't pay for extra service or better ambiance at a retail store, when they can buy the same products online or in local markets for much less.

Unlike in America where economies of scale for big-box retailers mean lower prices, smaller shops in China undercut big box retailers because they do not adhere to global business standards and have cheaper employee costs. Shop owners often live in back of stores or save costs by not using air conditioning or having dim lighting.

The result is that consumers will window-shop at big-box retailers for product information, but will buy online or in local electronics markets. Many consumers told us they would go to Best Buy's computer section to get objective, insightful advice from sales clerks who did not work on commission, but then go to smaller shops where they could buy the same computers for less and get pirated versions of software.

Home improvement chains Home Depot (from the United States) and La Maison (from France) made this mistake by selling the same items found in local decoration markets for higher rates, only to be seen as having high prices. They should have differentiated their product lines more. Both chains closed shop in China, and their British competitor, B&Q, is barely hanging on, having closed 50 percent of its stores.

Key Action Item

Retailers must differentiate their product selection from local competition in order to charge premiums, and to avoid becoming a destination where consumers go for education but not to purchase. If retailers fail to do so and try to compete on service, they will suffer from the perception of being higher priced, even if it isn't always true.

8

CHINESE NEO-COLONIALISM IN AFRICA AND THE END OF AMERICAN HEGEMONY?

The first African I met in China was a Rwandan named Gahiji studying Mandarin at Nankai University. I was downing some beer in the hot Tianjin night air in 1998 at a joint called Alibaba's, when I noticed a haunted-looking man hunched over at the table next to me. His appearance shocked me. He had purplish, craterlike scars all over his arms and legs. He wore a loose, mud-colored tank top, stained with sweat, over his chubby torso.

But it was his eyes that drew my attention to him—yellow, pit-like, almost lifeless. I watched him down 14 shots of vodka before he looked over at me and grunted for me to pull my stool over. When I came over, he started speaking to me in a drunken blend of Chinese, French, English, and what I later learned was Kinyarwanda. It was hard to understand what he was saying, but over the next few months I spent many nights drinking and talking with him, listening to his story and gradually piecing the fragments together.

Gahiji had ended up in China in the aftermath of the genocide in his home country four years earlier. One million Rwandans had been slaughtered in ethnic clashes in a six-week period, while the rest of the world did nothing. There was a deep pain in his voice (which I later noticed again during my talks with Lili Li), and during our discussions I thought to myself how lucky I was to have had a peaceful life growing up in America, and how chaotic some parts of the world can still be.

His story was tough to listen to. He told me how he saw his own son get hacked to death in front of him with a machete, pantomiming with his arm the thrust of a machete onto his son's skull as he spoke. He kept motioning in a slicing movement while mumbling, "My wife . . . hacked to death . . . my parents . . . my whole family murdered by Hutus in front of my eyes. There was no reason I survived. I wish I had not."

The pain and suffering Gahiji had dealt with just a few short years before shook me. When I hear relatives on my father's side of the family who are Jewish talk about the suffering during the Holocaust under the Nazis, it is hard for me to imagine. I tend to compartmentalize those images as things that happened long ago and far away, picturing them as grainy black-and-white photographs. Even when I visited Auschwitz as a teenager, it was hard to picture the horror that had taken place there; it was a sunny day and the death camp looked so peaceful and still.

But Gahiji was a real, live person in full color, just a few years older than me, who had gone through hell and was trying to crawl out.

As I got to know Gahiji, I learned that many other Tutsis like him had come to China to study on full scholarships, as had students from several other African countries. In the years since then, every time I have visited a major Chinese university to give a speech or meet with university officials, I have seen African students walking and biking around campus.

China's drive to attract African students was not driven by purely altruistic motivations. Even back in the 1990s, the Chinese government was making a push to build relationships with elite families all over Africa. Inviting well-connected Africans to study in China was part of an ongoing diplomatic battle with Taiwan. Both governments used loans, aid, and, likely, backroom business deals to secure official recognition as the true China. As a minor power back then, the People's Republic sought close relationships with small, nonaligned countries as a counterweight to American hegemony.

Another reason why the Chinese government opened up to African students was that, even in the 1990s, Chinese leaders were already attempting to smooth the path toward securing rights to the continent's abundant natural resources, especially oil and commodities like copper needed for construction, by cultivating relationships with leading African families. Countries that lack natural resources are subject to the whims of speculators, making them prone to inflation and derailing growth. History is rife with wars fought over resource access, and China does not want to get into a position where it feels caged in and has to use force to fight for oil or copper.

Today, China is garnering support not for international recognition of its statehood—it has already won that battle with Taiwan—but for the rights to Africa's natural resources and to disrupt American power, perhaps even to replace American dominance with its own form of world order. It has made this push by cooperating with local African elites, giving their children scholarships like the ones the Tutsis I met in Tianjin had received. In some administrations, scholarships are awarded to the children of nearly the entire government hierarchy.

One part of the deal is that China transfers technological knowhow and builds infrastructure projects like roads, highways, and bridges in African countries without the high-handedness of the colonial powers or America's moral campaigns. Unlike European countries and America, Chinese investment usually does not come with any conditions on things like governance. African elites have welcomed Chinese investment and trade, which is growing swiftly—Chinese trade with African countries is growing over 20 percent a year, and reached over $110 billion in 2011. Nearly one million Chinese workers now live in Africa, part of a massive influx of Chinese money to the African countryside.

Big infrastructure projects are what helped jumpstart China's own economic growth in the past few decades and cement its position as the dominant manufacturer, despite soaring labor costs. Many African countries have abundant natural resources, but sorely need infrastructure to enrich governments and spread the wealth to the general population. In a continent wracked by the lingering aftereffects of colonialism, despotic governments, disease, famine, and war, foreign investment is a far more useful tool for promoting real progress than foreign aid, and also far more sustainable. Charity does not pull countries and people out of poverty; improvement occurs when investment that creates jobs is made amid stable political climates.

In return, African governments give China's giant, state-owned mining companies long-term, secure access to precious commodities like Zambia's copper, Gabon's iron ore, and Angola's oil. China's government realizes that one of the few things that could derail its growth is lack of access to these key commodities. For this reason, since the financial crisis it has used its massive $3 trillion in foreign reserves to shore up deals in Africa and around the world, from Australia and Canada to Iraq and even Afghanistan.

Plans to further broaden Chinese involvement in Africa are constantly being proposed. Top officials, led by Premier Wen Jiabao and Robert Zoellick, the president of the World Bank, are discussing relocating factories that produce lower-value goods from southern China to Africa. While this will increase pollution in Africa, and unload jobs no longer desired by Chinese onto Africans, its countries needs the jobs and the hard currency. Chinese factory owners want to maintain a cheap source of labor, but know that they will no longer find it at home as workers there demand higher wages.

Chinese investment is not always welcomed by everyday Africans, many of whom view China as the latest in a long line of foreign interlopers with designs on plundering the continent. Many feel that they are laboring in mines or on infrastructure projects for little personal benefit. This relationship ironically mirrors the mentality of Chinese sweatshop factory workers 20 years earlier, when they produced sneakers and T-shirts catering to the American consumer. Other moves, like an attempt by a Chinese firm to acquire more than a 20 percent stake in Kenya Airways, have drawn protest from opposition party leaders, because such deals are seen as enriching and propping up the regime in power.

China became the main point of contention in Zambia's 2011 presidential election between the incumbent Rupiah

Banda, who welcomes Chinese investment, and opposition leader Michael Sata, who ran on an anti-China platform. Sata won because he wants to take a tougher line against Chinese investment, even though trade between the two nations grew from $100 million in 2000 to $2.8 billion in 2010. He called Chinese investors "infesters" and wants to expel Chinese migrant workers.

In the run-up to the election, violent riots took place in Zambia and at several Chinese-owned companies in other African nations, expressing the fear that African leaders are selling the countries' natural resources to China in a modern form of colonialism. In 2010, two Chinese coal mine executives in Zambia, while facing protests from local workers about pay and working conditions, fired shots into the crowd, wounding 11 people. The two managers were arrested and charged with attempted murder, but the charges were later dropped with no explanation from the Zambian government.

Dealing with the increasing mistrust of China's intentions on the part of average Africans is a problem Chinese enterprises and government will increasingly face in the future. China's companies and foreign-policy establishment will need to develop longer-term strategic thinking on how to deal with African nations. Too much of China's current foreign policy is predicated on the philosophy of "Don't interfere in our internal policy making and affairs, and we won't interfere in yours." As a core tenet of diplomacy, this might work for a minor power that wants to be friends with governments that don't want undue foreign influence, but not for an economic superpower with deepening interests in countries around the world.

For instance, because of its noninterference policy, China only recognized the Libyan National Transitional Council long after Western powers and even Russia acknowledged Gadhafi's overthrow. This has generated anger toward China among the new leadership in Tripoli.

AUSTRALIA

Chinese expansion is not just causing concern among politicians and local populations in Africa. China's grab for commodities has been particularly felt in Canada and Australia, whose deep reserves of iron ore and other resources are highly sought after by China.

I met Miranda and Abby, two law school students from Perth, Australia, who were taking advantage of a strong Aussie dollar to vacation in Thailand. Perth is one of the cities affected most by China's demand for iron ore because of the huge reserves in Western Australia and the Australian dollar has appreciated because of the demand.

Tanned with flowing blonde hair and a friendly smile, Miranda told me Chinese investment was driving prices in Perth through the roof. "It's now over seven Aussie dollars for a cup of coffee," she said—just over seven U.S. dollars. "Housing prices are going up and up—they're getting too high for most regular Australians." Abby, a brunette with athletic figure, told me a decent house now sells for 700,000 U.S. dollars, which is more than most people can afford, and that rising prices were making life difficult for too many people. *The Economist Intelligence Unit* reported in 2011 that Perth has become the 13th most expensive city in the world to live in. Five of the world's 25 most expensive cities are in Australia due to Chinese demand for its natural resources.

Miranda told me her family had benefitted from China's seemingly insatiable demand for iron ore. She welcomed the investment because the demand created high-paying jobs. Her father was an executive in the mining industry, and her dream job after graduation was to work at a white-shoe law firm for a few years before eventually shifting to an in-house legal position at a mining firm like Rio Tinto. The mining companies are where the money is, she said, and jobs there are more stable.

While Miranda and her family were benefiting from the mining boom, Abby was quick to point out the negative effects it was having on many of their fellow Australians. The mining wealth was not trickling down to the rest of the community, she said; the money brought in was concentrated among those in mining, while everyone else was being left behind.

Miranda agreed, saying local retailers were getting hit especially hard because the soaring Australian dollar was pushing consumers to shop online. Her friends were now taking advantage of a weak U.S. dollar to buy clothes from America. Even with shipping and handling, it was cheaper to go that route than to buy at a brick-and-mortar shop in Perth.

China's investments are creating friction between the haves and have-nots in Perth and in similar regions around the world, and are leading the government and its citizens to wonder whether Chinese money is a blessing or a curse.

This story is not unique to Australia. In 2010 I was eating lunch with one of Canada's most powerful members of Parliament. He turned to me and asked point-blank, "Should Canada welcome Chinese money? Is it a threat or an opportunity?"

He said that while he personally welcomed Chinese money to help create jobs, many of his constituents and the members of his party were worried about the security risks posed by Chinese firms' control of too many of Canada's natural resources. I heard this common theme from many leading Canadian politicians of different parties whenever I met them.

As China has outcompeted the West over the past few years, and doled out billions to buy up sovereign bonds in countries like Greece and Spain, countries around the world are beginning to wonder whether to put up barriers against Chinese money or to welcome it. By preventing too much Chinese investment, they hope to avoid security risks and the internal tensions created between those who benefit from Chinese money and those who do not. But they also worry about losing out on China's money and newfound power. The world's stock markets in the waning days of summer 2011 seemed to hinge on whether or not China would bail out Italy by buying its bonds, yet during the week when fears of an Italian collapse were highest, Italy was also trying to erect barriers to imports of Chinese ceramic tiles, which are cheaper and often of better quality than Italian ones.

"Canada is in a good position," the politician told me. "We can continue to explore more business opportunities with China, but our proximity to America lets us remain close. Other countries that aren't as close to America have harder decisions because they can't play that relationship off against China."

As China's might grows, nations around the world are going to have to decide how close to China they will get. Italy is a perfect example: It wants Chinese help, yet at the same is afraid that Chinese companies will take market share away from its biggest and most traditional industries.

One of the few things that can halt China's continuing explosive growth is the depletion of natural resources, which would cause steady, long-term inflation. For example, food prices soared throughout 2011, with year-over-year pork prices rising 50 percent, apples 30 percent, and yogurt 25 percent.

To try to keep a lid on raw-material inflation, China has adopted a forward-looking mind-set to build relationships with any country that will do business with it, regardless of ideology or human-rights issues. This has included working closely with countries like Sudan (both the southern and northern parts) and Iran, whose governments many Americans view as unsavory at best, and outright sponsors of terror at worst.

Many Western critics cite these ties as evidence of China's support of terrorism and genocidal regimes, which increases mistrust in Chinese leadership and its intentions. Western nations also fear these investments because they force the balance of international power away from America and disrupt the status quo. By investing abroad, and helping countries hit hard by the financial crisis by buying more of their bonds or products, China has won their support and gains more concessions in world affairs—but at the same time, this increases other countries' suspicion.

PAKISTAN

I met Tushna and Kaevan, a brother and sister from Karachi, Pakistan, in 2011. Kaevan had a bushy, jet-black mustache and short hair, and wore a brown shirt when we met over breakfast; his sister wore a light-red shirt.

As with many Pakistanis I have interviewed in the last decade, during which the United States used military bases in Pakistan to invade Afghanistan after September 11, there was frustration and sometimes anger in their voices about America's involvement in their country. They feel America has been arrogant and hypocritical in how it has dealt with Pakistan, and they are bitter about the Pakistani lives that have been lost.

Tushna put her cup of coffee on the table and said, angrily, "The Americans come and drop a bomb and kill civilians and act as if they are just casualties of war. Then when someone kills one of their soldiers, they act high and mighty as if it is morally wrong to kill." She continued, showing her annoyance: "When American leaders travel the city they shut entire roads for a day at a time, inconveniencing everyone. How can we live when we cannot go anywhere? How are they helping us?"

Tushna and Kaevan's anger was palpable. I was a little worried they would start yelling at me, as a group of Pakistanis once did in 2010, at a conference in Vietnam where I was a speaker, when they found out I am American. I decided to change the subject to China.

Immediately, a smile emerged from under Kaevan's mustache, and his whole body seemed to relax. "China has been an all-weather friend to us," he said. "Whether to help with security issues with India or problems with the United States, China has been there to support us rather than order us around." He rattled off the key areas of support China had provided to Pakistan since 1950, when Pakistan became one of the first nations to recognize China over Taiwan: key military aid, cooperation on building Pakistan's civilian nuclear power initiatives, and economic assistance.

Kaevan's sister agreed. "All levels of Pakistani society right now like China. They are bringing money without American arrogance. They don't tell us what to do as if we are children and don't know any better."

Many countries that have political systems other than American-style democracy, such as Pakistan, are naturally gravitating towards China, not only because of money but because they see China as being more hands-off about their internal affairs. For many Westerners, China's deals with regimes that are opposed to or ambivalent about American power gives them the impression that China lacks morality.

One of the issues China will have to deal with internally in the coming years is how to balance its need for natural resources and its newly found prominent position in world affairs. It is demanding more power in international organizations like the International Monetary Fund and the World Bank, where Chinese economists Zhu Min and Justin Lin have taken senior positions. Yet if it does this, it will also have to adhere to demands from the rest of the world for it to take a greater moral stand against injustice.

The crux of the issues surrounding China on an international scale is that the world does not fully comprehend how to deal with a rising China. In many ways, the financial crisis has put China in a position of power so quickly that other nations do not quite know how to handle this new situation. China also likes to hide its true power and intentions in order to gain more power, because other countries won't know exactly what they are dealing with. As a result, they often overestimate China's military capabilities.

One retired senior politician from America told me, "If China is increasing its trade volumes around the world, shouldn't it be securing its own shipping lanes?" He was irritated because he felt China was freeloading on the U.S. Navy's protection of maritime trade routes, but was taking an increasingly muscular stand in the South China Sea, causing anger in Vietnam and the Philippines.

AMERICA

On a trip to the United States in early 2011 to give a speech at the Wharton School of Business, I took my three-year-old son, Tom, to New York to see Times Square. I had heard about a major advertising campaign the Chinese government had launched on electronic billboards there to improve its image with the millions of tourists who pass through each year. The campaign was a major initiative the government had launched to combat increasing anti-China rhetoric in America, and the rising uneasiness that was accompanying China's emergence in places like Canada and Australia.

My son wouldn't stop jumping up and down until we tracked down the billboard. I had been telling him, during the incredibly slow Amtrak ride from Boston, about how cool the campaign would be. He was bubbling as if we were about to visit Disney World.

As soon as we arrived, we saw the famous Naked Cowboy playing his guitar on our right, but looking around we couldn't find the ad anywhere. I asked police officers if they knew where the China ads were. All shrugged their shoulders and said they didn't know.

After about an hour of walking around, eventually carrying Tom on my shoulders when he got tired, I finally found China's attempt at soft power. It was underwhelming to say the least.

The screen showing the commercial was tucked away on a poorly visible section of the square. Even worse, it was filled with shots of Chinese scientists, businessmen, athletes, and movie stars. With the exception of Yao Ming, there was nobody that anyone in Times Square that day would have recognized. I barely recognized most of them myself, and none really represented what China is to me. I stopped a woman walking by, whom I recognized as a mainlander, to ask if she knew the people in the ad. She said she recognized only a few.

The campaign was an utter failure. It failed to establish a connection with the American public and tourists from around the world, because it didn't understand at the most basic level who in China is known or unknown in America, or how views of China are shaped. The producers simply had not analyzed their target audience and therefore used the wrong images. Implicit in the attempt itself was at least an acknowledgment that China needs to show a better face to the world, but it also proved that it doesn't know how to do so yet.

If China is going to address the negative feelings bubbling up toward it throughout the world, it will need to do a better job than this, I thought. Most soft power needs to come from Chinese society itself, not necessarily through government-sponsored initiatives that are out of touch with everyday people in other nations.

It is the year 2030 in Beijing. A sinister-looking Chinese professor is teaching a class about the rise and fall of global powers in a dark lecture hall lined with Mao posters. The professor attributes America's downfall for his students, who are furiously taking notes, to overspending, tax hikes, and big government. He sneeringly lectures that China owned America's debt and concludes, "Now they work for us." The students cackle in response.

This was a TV ad titled "Chinese Professor," commissioned by Citizens Against Government Waste in the run-up to the 2010 U.S. midterm elections. It made headlines in America by evoking the fear of a world overrun with Chinese. During the 2010 campaign, at least 29 candidates from both parties tapped into American fears of China in an attempt to scare people into voting for them. Nevada Senator Harry Reid's campaign aired an ad accusing opponent Sharron Angle of being "a foreign worker's best friend" for supporting tax breaks to encourage outsourcing to China and India. An ad commissioned by Ohio Congressman Zack Space featured a sarcastic voice thanking

Republican opponent Bob Gibbs for supporting free-trade policies that sent Ohioans' jobs to China. American anti-China ads are only growing more sensational and direct; a 2011 ad paid for by former Nevada Republican Party chair Mark Amodei featured images of Chinese soldiers marching on the Capitol Building in Washington, DC.

Sadly, the anti-China rhetoric in U.S. political advertisements reflects the larger pattern of anti-Chinese headlines in the media. As mentioned, Paul Krugman has increased the bad feelings toward the Chinese government by arguing that it is directly stealing American jobs by keeping its currency artificially low. President Obama has accused China of not "playing by the rules."

Meanwhile, fears are rising in London about wireless hubs built by Chinese telecom maker Huawei. Many Londoners believe these systems allow the Chinese government to spy on them. Even the Committee of Foreign Investment in the United States advised Huawei to divest its acquisition of American server company 3Leaf Systems due to national security concerns. This recommendation came after Huawei had already paid $2 million for the intellectual property.

China has become an easy scapegoat as the United States suffers through a jobless economic recovery as well as attempts to cut spending and adjust the debt ceiling. It is far easier to blame China than to take responsibility for profligate spending by everyday Americans, poor oversight by regulators, irresponsible risk-taking by Wall Street financial institutions, and a bickering political class.

Every generation of Americans seems have its favorite bogeyman. In 1960s, it was Vietnam and the scourge of the godless Communist. In the mid-to-late 1980s, as relations with the Soviet Union warmed, Japan became the threat, especially after it bought iconic American landmarks like Rockefeller Center and Pebble Beach. Movies like the 1993 Sean Connery/Wesley Snipes thriller *Rising Sun*, based on the Michael Crichton novel, stoked U.S. fears of an America, Inc. already having been taken over by inscrutable Japanese.

Since then, with Japan's economy stagnant for two decades and China overtaking it as the world's second-largest economy, China has now replaced Japan as the threat. Many people like to draw parallels between Japan in the 1980s and China today, but these simple parallels ignore a few clear and important differences. In fact, Americans should be far more welcoming of Chinese investment.

Japanese companies believed in the superiority of their management system. Made confident by books such as Ezra Vogel's *Japan as Number One: Lessons for America,* Japanese executive teams felt they had developed new a new management technique that ought to replace the outdated American model. They thought their low executive salaries and family-like corporate atmospheres emphasized the company over the individual and bred more loyal and driven employees. American businessmen began reading works like *A Book of Five Rings* by Miyamoto Musashi and Chet Flippo's *New York Magazine* article "Samurai Businessman."

Japanese companies were ruthless with the foreign companies they bought out. They quickly replaced senior management teams and instituted glass ceilings for top positions. Even today, few Japanese companies in the United States have non-Japanese senior executives. Often the *gaijin* they do have are mere tokens, who do not have much power internally.

Soon after the explosion of the dot-com bubble, Ron, a 48-year-old Harvard Business School graduate who worked for a big Japanese bank in New York, told me, "The worst thing a high-achieving American can do is work at a Japanese firm. They put glass ceilings everywhere and you get treated like you're inferior. Once the economy gets better, I'm out of here."

Contrast this with Chinese companies. In interviews my firm conducted with senior executives of Chinese firms, they buy foreign companies for their brand equity, technology know-how, and, most important, their modern management systems. I don't think I have ever heard a Chinese businessman say he thought Chinese management systems were superior to American ones. One of the main goals of Chinese firms is to buy Western companies to learn from them.

When Chinese firms complete acquisitions, not only are most foreign management structures left untouched, but their best practices are often exported to China. China is constantly seeking to improve existing operations in the home market. Take, for instance, when Chinese computer maker Lenovo acquired IBM's ThinkPad laptop line. There were few layoffs, and Lenovo actually poached senior executives from Dell to run their operations. They did not install senior Chinese officials until the business lost market share in the domestic Chinese market and the founder of Lenovo took back the helm, much as Michael Dell did when Dell's business faced headwinds.

In other words, America should welcome investment from Chinese companies instead of fearing it. China is not looking to steal U.S. white-collar jobs and create a realm with limited opportunities for Americans. New economic connections between America and China can also hedge against security risks in the future. After World War II, America was able to rebuild its relations with Germany and Japan by integrating their economies with its own. This strategy worked well in the past and has the potential to work again in the present.

CHINESE SOFT POWER

The Chinese government's most impressive attempt at soft power to date has been the Confucius Institute program. It is a network of learning centers at Western universities, supported with funding from the Chinese government and aimed at promoting the Mandarin language and Chinese culture. Such a strategy works much better than the advertisement in Times Square; it caters directly to students and teaches them to appreciate Chinese culture.

This strategy still has some shortcomings, however. While this program gets young people excited about the prospects of living and working in China, the government has recently clamped down on issuing visas to young foreigners. By being so strict, it frustrates and potentially alienates students who are genuinely passionate about China and want to work there. I personally offered a job to a young Penn State graduate who was excited about working in China. His father owned a restaurant business there, and he was thrilled at the prospect of starting his career there, too. Unfortunately, we were unable to secure a visa for him, which left him frustrated.

Although it has lost the struggle for diplomatic recognition, Taiwan has been much more successful than the People's Republic at using soft power. Taiwan's government has paid for Mandarin language training and research stipends for many of America's leading professors and graduate students through the Chiang Ching-kuo Foundation, which in turn often takes the Taiwanese view in its struggle with the mainland. As China rises in the world, it must become more adept at using its soft power—and it will.

When I was the assistant director of the Centre for East Asian Research at McGill University during the late 1990s, I spent a lot of time raising funds for the university's programs, as well as traveling to counterpart universities around the world. The South Korean government supports film festivals in universities around North America through the Korea Foundation. They also pay for academic conferences, events, and faculty support. A large part of the funding for McGill's robust Korean studies program came from the Korea Foundation. This was a great way to build support for South Korea, be it political support or a continued military presence to combat volatility in the North.

The Taiwanese also were very generous, mostly through private foundations and often with direct or tacit support of the government. The Chiang Ching-kuo Foundation, named after Chiang Kai-shek's son, who became supreme leader of Taiwan after his father died, supported professors' active academic research. Nearly all of my professors who were over 45 years old had spent their formative years studying China and Mandarin either in Taiwan or backed by Taiwanese money.

Private foundations also financially supported such people as my Harvard classmate Wang Dan, who was one of the student leaders during the Tiananmen protests in 1989. Wang Dan has continued to be one of China's foremost critics. Backed by Taiwanese money with specific agendas, he will be unlikely to voice anything but opposition to China.

This cooptation of the academic class and its students, which has a trickle-down effect that affects policies governing military exchanges and weapons sales, helps Taiwan advance its agenda. China, on the other hand, is poor at this and does not have a strong lobbying effort within the Western world.

China needs to start funding more academic research and exchange. They should also promote the establishment of foundations using private Chinese money. Too much of China's soft power has been government controlled and led. As Chinese become wealthier, many of them want to help promote China's image to the world through their own funding and initiatives.

The government needs to make it easier to set up nongovernmental organizations (NGOs). It is far too afraid of them, which stems from worries that they cannot be controlled and might be fronts through which foreign government will create subversion. The process to establish them should be made easier. Besides, the government has admitted that 90 percent of NGOs operating in China don't have legal licenses; many simply register as businesses.

Many debates in China focus on how it should build its image abroad. This is extremely important, as we have seen in Africa, where people's perception of China can potentially determine the future of its relations there. Historically, Chinese leaders have strived to maintain issues of national sovereignty as the paramount focus of their foreign diplomacy. The idea is that the Chinese government won't intervene in other nations' affairs, with the expectation that, in turn, no one will inquire into theirs. The Chinese government is good at rattling cages to gain more influence during international discussions, but shies away from taking too large an international role in actual decision making. In the mind of the Chinese government, it is better to spend money on its internal needs, and to let America waste its money acting as the world's policeman.

Harnessing and asserting its soft power is China's best bet; however, it must do a better job. The government recognizes this, and has been spending serious money to promote China's good name worldwide. Unfortunately, many of their attempts so far have failed to improve China's brand position.

As the End of Cheap China increases consumption and the demand for better-quality housing and jobs, China's need for natural resources will only get bigger. Further investment abroad will naturally cause more tension.

CASE STUDIES
WHAT TO DO AND WHAT NOT TO DO IN CHINA

• Do Not Fear the Chinese as the Japanese Were Feared

Cash-rich Chinese companies, like state-owned Bright Food or privately owned Fosun Group, have been on buying sprees scooping up Western brands. This trend has spurred concerns in the Western world that Chinese firms will acquire companies and then fire scores of workers or implement glass ceilings, much as Japanese companies did in the 1980s with non-Japanese executives.

These worries are exaggerated, because Chinese and Japanese firms view the acquisition process differently. Chinese firms tend to acquire companies to buy brands for introduction into China, to cut the time needed for building brands, and to import technological know-how and management expertise. Unlike Japanese firms, they are less likely to cut the senior management of acquired companies or block the advancement of executives who are not native Chinese.

For instance, when Chinese computer maker Lenovo acquired the IBM ThinkPad line, it installed an American chief executive officer. The chairman of Bright Food, which has bought stakes in companies such as Australia's Manassen, announced that they would keep senior management in place to learn from them. Similarly, when Chinese auto manufacturer Geely bought the Swedish Volvo brand, it also retained senior management and took a comparatively hands-off approach to Volvo's operations.

When Western companies are acquired by Chinese ones, executives should expect some culture shock, because the chairmen and founders of large Chinese companies tend to be more hands-on and delegate less than heads of American firms. Many decisions can only be made when the chairman himself gives the go ahead. But overall, the process will be less unsettling than acquisitions by Japanese firms in the 1980s.

Key Action Item

Selling to a Chinese firm might be a good way to improve company valuation yet retain key leadership positions. It will also help companies gain better distribution channels into China, which are costly and hard to build for Western firms. Before selling to a Chinese company, instead of preparing for glass ceilings or massive layoffs, you should anticipate a culture clash owing to the more hands-on management style of Chinese firms' founders and chairmen.

• Chinese Go Abroad to Shop

Many brands set up huge stores in China that remain devoid of shoppers, yet still report huge sales to mainland-Chinese consumers. How does that happen? The answer is simple: Chinese consumers prefer to travel abroad to shop, especially for premium and luxury items. Not only is it cheaper to shop abroad, because China slaps 20 to 30 percent tariffs and value-added taxes on imported goods, but it is also more prestigious to buy a Cartier watch in Paris than in Beijing. In interviews with five large luxury chains, executives told my firm that their sales to mainland-Chinese consumers in international locations are growing faster than sales within China. Brands like Omega have opened up museums and display areas in China, but channel sales through multiple outlets in Hong Kong. In this way, brands might want to target Chinese consumers in China with store fronts and advertising campaigns, but should expect to actually close sales abroad.

Key Action Item

VIP programs and sales targets should be integrated between China-based and foreign offices. When the Chinese branch of a firm tries to take back market share from foreign branches, it creates too much internal competition. Consumers have also told my firm that they got upset when brands' VIP loyalty programs are specific to a certain country rather than to the brand worldwide.

- Prepare Your American and European Shops for Chinese Tourists

One spring day, I found myself in New York City again, walking along Fifth Avenue, interviewing salespeople at stores like Louis Vuitton and Gucci. I asked around in these stores what the Chinese consumer presence had been recently. The sales clerks all said that mainland-Chinese shoppers account for 60 percent of luxury item sales, while Brazilians account for 20 percent. Just five years ago, the majority of sales were to Americans. Today, the average Chinese tourist spends $7,000 per trip to the United States. They are also the highest-spending tourists per capita in France.

To attract more sales, therefore, brands should hire Mandarin-speaking sales clerks, much as many retailers on the Gold Coast in Australia and Maui in Hawaii hired Japanese-speaking staff in the 1980s.

The British retailer Harrods announced that their sales to affluent Chinese in the first quarter of 2011 soared 40 percent after they installed 75 ATMs that accept UnionPay cards, which let shoppers deduct funds directly from their bank accounts in China.

Similarly, Hilton Hotels & Resorts announced that in 50 key hotels around the world, they would have one Mandarin-speaking front-desk clerk to welcome Chinese guests, and would have slippers and tea kettles, to which Chinese are accustomed, available in rooms. Hilton will also localize breakfast menus by offering congee and other items that make up traditional Chinese breakfasts.

Key Action Item

To attract well-heeled Chinese consumers travelling abroad, companies need to add aspects that Chinese consumers specifically like to their offerings, and introduce Mandarin-speaking staff as Hilton is doing.

9

CHINA'S EDUCATIONAL SECTOR

PREVENTING CHINA FROM CEMENTING
ITS SUPERPOWER STATUS

I was sitting in an oak-paneled meeting room in a five-star Beijing hotel. Surrounding me were several dozen of China's smartest and most-talented teenagers and their anxious parents. They were there to interview for a leading boarding school in the United States, and I was there to take my niece to interview.

As we waited, the teenagers asked me about my own experiences decades before as a boarding-school student at St. Paul's School, the preparatory school in Concord, New Hampshire, that has graduated artists like *Doonesbury* cartoonist Garry Trudeau, government officials like Senator John Kerry and FBI Director Robert Mueller, and business titans like former

Mitsubishi Chairman Minoru Makihara. While I was there, Tim Ferriss, the best-selling author of *The 4-Hour Work Week* and *The 4-Hour Body*, was my classmate.

One young man with the broad shoulders of a lumberjack came up to me and asked, "Are class sizes better in boarding schools in America than in China? There are fifty people in my class at my school in Beijing now—it is way too big." He continued to ask me about curriculum choices and whether there were electives. Next to him stood a slightly pudgy, pimply-faced girl dressed in a plaid skirt and a white, buttoned blouse. She strode up close to me and asked, "Can you please tell me about the extracurricular activities? Can I go horseback riding? How about golf? All the choices are so exciting."

These students represented the best of China, and they represented it well. They would be the ones changing the face of the country and the world in a few short years, and they seemed to know it. They were not timid, as many Westerners think Chinese youths are, and had no qualms about asking questions, even though I was a foreigner and much older.

These young people were far more worldly and sophisticated than I was 20 years earlier when I was interviewing for boarding school. I was obsessed with baseball cards and Madonna at their age, while these kids discussed Plato and Hemingway. Their fascination with the American way of life was apparent when they discussed why a class size of 8 to 12 in an American institution was superior to 50 students in a top Chinese school, or why being able to make art and play team sports, even if they were not very talented, was an exciting prospect.

As I answered the dozens of questions they asked me, I was encouraged by the quality of the students and their probing inquiries. China was most assuredly raising young adults who had thought-provoking questions, such as one young man, dressed in a navy blue suit with gold buttons, who asked me about how I saw China's role emerging in the world. After I answered, he offered his own opinion: that China's rise would be peaceful and would help raise more people out of poverty through business investment.

However, one big problem stuck in the back of my mind as we talked: All these kids wanted to leave China for their education, because its current educational system is failing the country.

As my niece was interviewing, I struck up a conversation with some of the parents. Mr. Chen, a billionaire real estate developer whose firm puts up towering skyscrapers all over the country, pulled up a chair next to me. He wore a diamond-encrusted Omega watch, but he looked a little rumpled; although his clothes were all from extremely high-end luxury brands and must have cost a fortune, they did not seem to fit him right.

Mr. Chen let out a deep, guttural cough, the result of far too many years of smoking or working in China's old factories. He told me he was conflicted about his choice to educate his daughter overseas. He was reluctant to send his daughter so far away, but at the same time, he admitted to me, "We have to send our child abroad. The Chinese education system is focused too much on rote memory and not how to think, does not emphasize moral reasoning, and does not have extracurricular activities to allow a child to become well rounded."

Out of the corner of my eye, I could see the other parents nodding in agreement. Mr. Chen continued, "Why shouldn't our children learn art and drama? Why shouldn't they play team sports, even if they won't be the next Yao Ming? Why is everything focused on test preparation and how to make money? There has to be more to life than just money."

These parents were people who had benefitted the most from reforms since the end of the Cultural Revolution. They were the sons and daughters of high government officials, wealthy businessmen, and famous celebrities. These were supporters of the government, yet they planned to send their children out of China to get a good education. It seemed like they all feared for their children's futures if they didn't send them abroad to study, unless immediate changes could be implemented to China's education system. In a survey of three dozen wealthy Chinese with investable assets more than $10 million, my firm found the majority are obtaining foreign passports or thinking about it, not because they dislike the government but because it opens up more educational opportunities for their children.

One of China's greatest challenges is reforming its one-dimensional education system. It simply does not adequately prepare Chinese young people for the challenges and opportunities they will face in the global marketplace and in a country that is shifting toward a more service-based economy. Successful business executives, teachers, and government officials will not be created by educational systems that only teach students how to take tests and memorize answers, but by learning how to evolve and adapt quickly to changing conditions.

The problem is not merely academic, nor is it one that only has repercussions for the distant future. The problem is already hitting China's business community and Chinese society in general. The educational system teaches students how to memorize the right answer, but doesn't train them to have the creativity to develop a new right answer. As I wrote in Chapter 2, multinational corporations have told my firm that the biggest problem they face in China is recruiting and retaining labor, in part because of the weak talent pool.

As jobs become rely more upon brainpower than muscle power, companies are desperate to hire top people—yet nearly 15 percent of the more than six million fresh 2010 university graduates could not find a job several months after graduation. One Shanghai-based senior executive at a multinational financial-services firm told me with frustration, "Graduates just don't know how to think analytically. They are great at doing what they are told to do, but they are terrible when it comes to creating something and taking initiative. We have to hire—we've even lowered our standards to do so—but we can't hire people who cannot think."

There is an obvious mismatch between the demands of the job market and the aspirations of China's youth on the one hand, and the skills provided by the educational system on the other. The government, to its credit, has been increasing access to higher education as it recognizes that the long-term strength of a country rests with an educated workforce. The number of annual university graduates has soared from one million 15 years ago to more than six million in 2010 from over 2,000 universities. Only about 30 percent of high school graduates continue on to college in China—low as compared with 70 percent in the United States, but quite good for a country with a massive population whose universities were all shut just 40 years ago.

The growth in the number of university graduates, however, is no indicator of the quality of the education they are receiving. The standard class size is too large, so there is no individual attention in the classroom, and teachers must emphasize rote memorization and test grades to standardize the system. Individual schools are not allowed to change the curriculum at all, so there is no focus on the method of learning, only upon exam results or changes for different levels of academic achievement.

For this reason, there is little classroom interaction and next to no emphasis on critical thinking.

The college entrance examination, the *gaokao,* is central to the problems between the Chinese education system and the job market. After high school, students who hope to attend the country's universities sit for several days straight taking the test that will determine which school they will attend and the major they will study. It is an extraordinarily crucial moment in their lives. Because the exam is only administered once a year, this is a nerve-wracking experience, and the entire country quiets down as students prepare. Construction stops. Car horns go silent, and police are out in force to stop any noise that might bother test takers. The whole country understands the importance of these tests, and in unified solidarity people will inconvenience themselves on students' behalf.

Unlike the application process in America, high school grades, leadership, and extracurricular efforts are not taken into account unless a student is an extremely brilliant talent. Only prestigious academic awards, or an exceptional offer of matriculation without examination, relieve a student from the stress of the gaokao. Gaining admission without taking the test is an incredibly elite route, and most students don't enter this way.

The high stress levels it imposes on students and society, and its narrow focus on the results of a single exam, are not the only flaws of the gaokao system. It also forces students to select the major they want to study and the university they want to attend before even taking the test. Government-set quotas and higher enrollment qualifications for different majors lead students to choose majors for all the wrong reasons. Often the choice is not based on genuine interest, but rather on the likelihood that the student will achieve the cutoff score for a given major. For example, some highly competitive majors, like international finance or world economy, require higher entrance test scores than less competitive majors like literature. This is very different from the American way, which uses general aptitude tests as a standard for every university, regardless of major.

As a result, in order to enter a prestigious domestic university, students often commit themselves to the wrong major for four years. One student I met named Helen told me she pursued Middle Eastern studies at the prestigious Peking University not because she wanted to, but because it was the department with the lowest required test scores, and she really wanted to go to Peking University to make her parents proud. After she graduated—hating her area of study by that point—Helen went to the United Kingdom as soon as she could to pursue a master's degree in business.

Additionally, students often enter a university unprepared to make sound decisions about their future course of study, and frequently apply to majors like accounting because a relative or family friend suggested it as a stable and suitable career. For the next four years, these students are forced to study a major they probably knew very little about when they applied. After all, when I applied to university I wrote in my college essays that I wanted to become an anthropologist and study in the Congo. That dream went out the door my first day at McGill University in Montreal, when I ended up in a Chinese-studies class and fell in love with Chinese paintings.

For the select few who get into a university, there is little to no flexibility to change your course of study. There is also almost no room to take any electives outside of your chosen department. This means that Chinese universities are graduating people who spend four years learning about biology or accounting and nothing else. It produces classes full of students who are arguably good at one discipline, but who are unable to synthesize any outside information into their narrow frame of reference. This is a crippling flaw for those hoping to succeed in today's fast-paced and integrated world.

Sitting in front of my desk was a young woman named Mimi, 1 of 10 applicants for an entry-level position at my firm out of 2,000 graduates in 2007 who made it to the final round of the interview process. She wore a conservative, dark-blue suit that matched her plain face, and was so tall that she made the chair she was sitting in look like a toy. She had on a wristwatch with a cartoon face. I think it was Hello Kitty.

Mimi was about to graduate from the famed Shanghai Jiao Tong University, where former President Jiang Zemin went to school, with a degree in accounting. As she fidgeted in the chair and kept moving her legs to get into a more comfortable position, I asked her why she was interested in market research rather than accounting—after all, the big accounting firms like KPMG, PricewaterhouseCoopers, and Deloitte were adding thousands of positions a year.

She immediately stopped moving around and answered quite directly, "I applied for accounting at Shanghai Jiao Tong as a major because my mother's friend thought it was a good career path for a girl, so I checked the box. I had no idea what accounting was. After my first class, I hated it and wanted to try something else, but I wasn't allowed to change majors. I like CMR because I like the idea of working on an apparel project one day, a hedge fund due-diligence project another day, and a chemical project the next. I need a more broad-based understanding of the business world. I want to get as far away from accounting as possible."

Mimi's response was similar to so many I had heard in interview after interview. Few people told me that they liked their major; they had chosen it for all the wrong reasons many years ago, and usually hated it. For their first career step, they all seemed to want a job that would gave them broad exposure, because they were tired of looking at the same area over and over again.

I liked Mimi, but ultimately we did not hire her. Despite her earnest wish to expand her mind, she seemed unable to think creatively in our interviews.

Notwithstanding these problems, many parents in America wrongly believe China's educational system is still far superior to America's because of its unique ability to breed test takers. The *New York Times* reported in late 2010 that Shanghai's high school students performed better than American high school students on a standardized test administered by the Organisation for Economic Co-operation and Development, the Program for the International Student Assessment. Many in America took the test results as proof that American students were lagging behind Chinese students in ability and that China's system is far superior. U.S. Secretary of Education Arne Duncan said he saw the test scores as a "wake-up call" for America. In a misguided column for the *Washington Post*, Vivek Wadhwa argued that America needs to "fear" China's youngsters graduating from Chinese universities, because they will use their innovative abilities to start competing against Silicon Valley's greatest minds.

However, test scores do not measure an understanding of information or the ability to use it to develop something useful. They are merely a tool to quantify and standardize a child's performance in a certain pool of students. Moreover, Wadhwa's examples of top Chinese were actually Taiwanese and ethnically Chinese Americans who studied in America.

Proof that the American educational system still trumps the Chinese one is in the admission numbers, not the test scores. Since China opened up in the last 30 years, one million Chinese students have studied abroad. In the last five years, more than 30 percent have returned to China.

More and more Chinese will study outside the country as Chinese families become wealthier and begin to send their children abroad at an earlier age, like the students I met during my niece's private-school interview. These parents want to expand their children's awareness of the world, not unlike programs run by American universities for students to spend a year abroad. Another, more practical reason is that parents think that holding a prestigious foreign degree will make their children better candidates in the Chinese job market. Eighty percent of my firm's Chinese hires in the last three years went abroad to get master's degrees before returning to start their careers in China.

Parent after parent tells me the main reason they send their child abroad is their lack of faith in the Chinese educational system. Even China's top leaders send their children abroad. The daughter of Xi Jinping, China's presumptive next president after Hu Jintao, is an undergraduate at Harvard. The grandchildren of past leaders like Hu Yaobang, Chen Yun, Deng Xiaoping, and Bo Yibo all studied at Yale, Harvard, and Duke. Can you imagine Barack Obama sending his daughters abroad for their undergraduate studies? If the very top of Chinese society is looking abroad for education, it is clear something is lacking at home, no matter what the test scores, or alarm by pundits like Wadhwa, indicate.

• • •

After the Cultural Revolution, when many scholars were harassed and universities' doors were shut, China's intellectual capital was so far behind in terms of innovation and entrepreneurship that the government actively promoted leading scholars' studies abroad. They hoped that Chinese students would bring Western management prowess and technological knowledge back to China. For example, they sent the scholar Zhu Min to America, where he received a doctorate at Johns Hopkins University before returning home. He now is the Deputy Managing Director of the International Monetary Fund. Many of my Chinese classmates from Harvard are now working for the government or have high-paying academic positions at elite universities like Peking University.

Even with the number of scholars the government sent abroad, China's skill set is still far too weak. Companies recognize this educational deficit in their Chinese workers, and are spending massive portions of their budgets on internal training. My firm interviewed 100 human resource officials at large and medium-sized companies in Beijing, Hangzhou, and Shanghai in late 2010. The vast majority said they were increasing their training budgets by 30 percent a year because their frontline executives were demanding better-trained and more highly qualified talent. One human resource executive in a state-owned oil company told me, "Our people are not trained well enough." He repeated a common joke, "We have great hardware but bad software," referring to human capital at his company. He told us he was planning to spend more on employee training, because the major problem keeping his company from achieving higher profits was the lack of qualified executives.

Young professionals are even willing to pay out of their own pockets to compensate for perceived skill-set deficiencies and to become more competitive for higher bonuses and salaries. Out of several hundred 24- to 28-year-olds in Shanghai, Guangzhou, and Beijing, 70 percent told my firm in 2008 that they would be willing to spend 10 percent or more of their disposable income on extra training and education. An astounding 10 percent responded they would be willing to pay 20 percent or more. One junior analyst at an information-services firm told me he was spending the equivalent of four months' salary on English classes at night because he needed to have better foreign-language skills to communicate with colleagues at his company's headquarters overseas. "I took English in school since I was five years old, but I still cannot talk well," he said to me with an odd accent that I could not quite place. "I learned my English from a Russian."

The demand for better-trained white collar workers will only increase as the population ages and the economy shifts from manufacturing and exports to domestic consumption and services. Although Chinese companies and graduates themselves are spending money and resources to make up for their lack of applicable skills, these channels are merely short-term fixes. China needs to establish a better educational system, starting from pre-kindergarten all the way through postdoctoral programs. It must create its own centers of excellent learning if China is to grow into and maintain international superpower status. Under the current educational system, this position cannot be attained.

All of the great superpowers have had bastions of learning that attracted the world's best students. When the British ruled the world, students flocked to Eton and Oxford. America has St. Paul's and Harvard. China currently has . . . nothing. The government needs to implement a stronger educational system, not only to train its own citizens, but also to draw top students from abroad. Achieving this level of international prestige is China's best chance to create a strong source of soft power, and will be far more effective than any advertising campaign in Times Square or on CNN. Foreign students studying in China will not only bring Chinese know-how back to their home countries, but also a respect for and understanding of Chinese values, culture, and way of life.

Why doesn't the government reform the system more swiftly? Even though everyone knows there is a problem, it will not be easy. Not a single Ministry of Education official or teacher I have spoken with has admitted to liking the current system, and often they, too, try to send their children abroad to study.

Part of the problem with reform is that the system is geared toward reducing corruption and ensuring that everyone has a fair shot at entering a university, no matter how humble the student's background. The educational bureau tries to guarantee the highest objectivity possible for university admittance. Test scores are seen as the most transparent measurement of ability, which is the reason why they are the sole determinant of college entrance in China. Officials and the Chinese people fear that the establishment of Western-style college admission committees will only invite corruption, with parents bribing admissions committees and teachers and using as many of their connections as possible to ensure their children enter the right schools. This form of corruption already occurs with admissions to leading primary and high schools.

Another roadblock for China's educational improvement is the immense number of people it must educate. In 2005 I had a business meeting at Zhejiang University, one of the more famous universities in the country, which is located in Hangzhou, the capital of Zhejiang Province in eastern China.

I took a slow, crowded train with my colleague Joe. We had an appointment to meet Ministry of Education and senior university officials to help them figure out strategies for dealing with overcrowding in classrooms.

Upon arrival, Joe and I were ushered into a room where we met a man named Professor Zhou. He was one of the first graduates from a Chinese university after schools reopened, following their closure for 10 years during the Cultural Revolution. He had experienced firsthand how poor policies at the top affected the whole country.

We sat down and started to drink lukewarm afternoon tea. Because there was no air conditioner, only a dingy, wheezing fan, our clothes clung to our backs with sweat. Between sips of tea and drags from a cigarette he gripped tightly in his bony hand, Professor Zhou began to explain his problems.

"We literally have class sizes of seven thousand students," he lamented while smoking away in his office. I thought my Chinese was failing again, so I suggested his university look into implementing an e-learning system that could easily cover 700 students. I tried to show him how the system could automate test-score grading, when Professor Zhou grabbed my arm with his bony hand in midsentence.

"No. No. No," he said adamantly, "I said seven thousand students. We have students connected by closed-circuit television."

Seven thousand in one class. That is more than the entire student body at many universities in America—larger than a lot of U.S. towns, in fact. The size of that single class shows the magnitude of the issue China faces, in the educational system as well as society at large: how to deal with a population so large.

Many Western observers have difficulties grasping the sheer scale of China's population or the implications of such population density on everything from housing and food to social instability. The population of China is five times larger than America's, but the vast majority live squashed together in a land area roughly the size of America's Eastern Seaboard. Much of the rest of the country, like the Gobi and Taklamakan Deserts and the Himalayas in Tibet, is uninhabitable.

For Professor Zhou's university, the government's efforts to give more people better access to education have manifested themselves in massive overcrowding and a subpar education system. The government wrestles with the dilemma of balancing increasing the quality of education with expanding its availability. As I left Professor Zhou that day, he told me that the situation would get better, but probably not anytime soon.

The government is directing major funding to leading universities like Professor Zhou's in their hope of fixing the system. They are actively recruiting Chinese professionals who have studied in America with pay packages rivaling those of American universities. Many of my graduate school classmates at Harvard are now teaching at universities in China, drawn by the chance to work in their homeland, but also because of the perks they are being awarded. They are given comfortable housing at heavily subsidized rates and huge research budgets, and are expected to bring international fame to their universities and to China.

Even one of my professors at Harvard University, famed Confucian scholar Du Weiming, left his position at Harvard to establish centers at Peking University and Zhejiang University.

Investing resources and recruiting international educators are great first steps in reforming the broken system, but at the end of the day, reforms need to focus on how and what students are taught. Intellectual capital needs to be spread throughout the entire population, not just the elite ranks.

Everyone acknowledges the problems, but figuring out how to fix them is more complicated. Switching from an objective, exam-based system to one that looks at more subjective metrics is fraught with the danger of increasing corruption. Parents whose children might do poorly from changes to the status quo will become angry and protest—another potential source of discord. This situation will only be exacerbated if admissions-corruption scandals engulf the country. More and better teachers need to be recruited, via improved benefits and training, to teach smaller class sizes in a more engaging, interactive format.

In order to progress, China needs to take into account what should be done and what can be done. The government needs to allow local ministry officials to collaborate with school officials to choose the educational materials used in class. It also should allow for more private schools answerable to the Ministry of Education that will be able to choose their own curricula pending ministry approval. These new institutions would create a space for foreigners and locals to study together. At the university level, the leading schools should provide a more liberal-arts-oriented education, and give students the freedom to choose majors after entering university and take electives.

All of these changes need to be made slowly, but the country cannot afford to go slowly. As China moves beyond being a low labor and real estate costs, and rises to economic-superpower status, it will need strong government officials, business leaders, entrepreneurs, and researchers to sustain its growth and solidify its global position. Human capital forms the backbone of long-term growth. To develop its next generation, China needs to establish learning centers of international excellence, invest resources appropriately, switch to a more subjective and diverse curriculum and entrance criterion, and open up greater access to education. China's problems with the quality and coverage of its education system are multifaceted, and many of its aspects need to be reformed to keep young talent within the country, where they will be needed to develop innovative solutions to meet its future challenges.

CASE STUDIES
WHAT TO DO AND WHAT NOT TO DO IN CHINA

- Take Advantage of Economic Inefficiencies

  Many parts of the economy, especially ones dominated by state-owned enterprises, remain inefficient because senior executives are often better at moving up the political ladder than earning profits. This leaves an opening for private enterprise to cater to consumer demands and move quickly to take market share away from lumbering, state-owned giants.

  For instance, according to our research, many state-owned banks like ICBC and Bank of China focus more on their business dealings with other state-owned enterprises, leaving private companies and retail consumers highly dissatisfied with their service. China Merchants Bank recognized this and concentrated heavily on delivering better service for high-net-worth individuals and credit card holders. The company has since become the dominant credit card player. Consumers give it one of the highest satisfaction levels of any Chinese company about which my firm has conducted surveys.

  Similarly, one of the last major sectors to undergo meaningful reform in China is the education and training sector. The government has not been able to reform the educational system swiftly enough to keep up with demands for more education in business skills.

Savvy training and education companies like New Oriental or EF Education fill this void by setting up learning centers that directly target consumers, such as young workers and parents of schoolchildren, who have the income to spend more on training themselves or their children.

Key Action Item

While many state-owned enterprises like China Mobile receive high satisfaction levels from consumers, many are still lumbering yet highly profitable giants because of political patronage. They are unable to move quickly enough to grab new sources of revenue, leaving huge openings for consumer-centric and fast-moving companies.

• Immigration

More wealthy Chinese are obtaining foreign citizenship. Why this is has stirred a national debate, with many foreign observers arguing it is because of dissatisfaction with the government. In interviews with 50 wealthy Chinese who obtained foreign passports or have thought about it, the vast majority said they would continue their business operations in China.

Their top reasons for wanting a foreign passport were ease of travel, better education and health care facilities, and worries over the effects of pollution on their families. Few, even among those who had already moved abroad, pointed to dissatisfaction with the government as one of their top reasons for securing a passport.

This shift abroad represents huge opportunities for foreign businessmen, from setting up housing complexes and restaurants that cater to Chinese tastes, to offering banking and education services in Chinese. Tabor Academy, a leading preparatory school in Massachusetts, even offers its application forms in Chinese.

Key Action Item

More and more Chinese will invest abroad to secure foreign passports. Many will move their families to other countries for the health benefits while retaining business operations in China, which creates opportunities for businesses to cater to them.

10

WHAT THE END OF CHEAP CHINA MEANS FOR THE REST OF THE WORLD

In September 2011, I flew to Paris to meet with the chief executive officers of some of the world's leading luxury brands. They had all seen soaring sales to Chinese consumers, and were eager to know more about the habits of China's ultrarich. In just a decade, China has emerged from being a money-losing backwater for luxury brands to become the world's second-largest luxury market. Chinese consumers have become the Japanese of the 1980s; wherever they travel, they shop for Louis Vuitton, Gucci, and Chloé, as well as a taste of the high life. Whole industries developed alongside Japan's rise—from duty-free shops in airports to sushi bars sprouting up wherever Japanese businessmen travelled—and fortunes were made. Traveling Chinese tourists and businessmen could inspire the same phenomena.

Even middle-class Chinese aspire to buy luxury products, as Japanese housewives did before. It is not uncommon to see secretaries who make $800 a month buying $1,000-dollar Gucci bags. They, too, will spark new cottage industries around the world for businesses smart enough to understand their needs.

As I walked along the Champs-Élysées, Chinese tourists were everywhere, rushing to Lancel and other elite brands' flagship stores. Seemingly every other person in the Louis Vuitton store was Chinese. Sales clerks there told me that Chinese were driving so much of the sales of the most popular and expensive items, that they had to limit the number of best-selling items each person could buy. My hotel—the ultra-opulent Shangri-La, Paris's latest five-star property—was full of Chinese businessmen and tourists with their hands full of shopping bags.

With the shadow of the debt crisis looming over Italy and Greece, people asked me during nearly every meeting I had while in Paris, "Will China save Europe?" At the time, investors were hoping China would be the white knight to bail Italy out by buying its bonds. Even the rumor that China might step in to buy them caused global equity markets to rebound.

Two camps have formed in world opinion on how to view China's rise, especially since it has emerged relatively unscathed from the financial crisis. One camp—which would include most businessmen, like those senior executives I met in Paris, and investors hoping for a China-led bailout of Italy and the rest of Europe—views China's rise as beneficial and a potential savior of the global economy and their own businesses. They want to make money, and do not really care about ideological battles. More economic integration is good, they reason, not only because it generates more profits, but it lessens the risk of tension and war, as interrelated economies and aligned interests force people to come together.

They remind others that international economic frameworks like the World Trade Organization minimize military conflicts like those that consumed the world just a few decades ago. They also adhere to the view that companies and countries constantly need to evolve and innovate to seize advantages in changes in the world, rather than erecting tariffs and other trade barriers in order to maintain their strength. This group tends to view China as a mix of white knight and mystical superhero who can magically save the world's economy and increase global security.

The other camp views China's rise as a zero-sum game that will negatively impact the Western world's ideological and economic dominance. They fear that China is a job stealer that manipulates currency in a mercantilist economic policy, and that it is a potential military enemy, to the detriment of America. They also feel that the Communist ideological strain in China, and the nation's stance on human rights, are misguided at best but most likely evil, and that both threaten the American way of life. The ranks of this group are a hodgepodge of differing ideologies, including leading liberal economists like Paul Krugman and union leaders along with more militant hawks.

Containing China's growth and influence in global affairs forms the bedrock of these China hawks. They have always had a suspicious eye on China, but they were distracted by September 11 and leading the Afghan and Iraq wars. Now that those wars are coming to a close, or lingering with less importance, these hawks are refocusing their attentions on China.

People holding anti-China opinions are gaining more currency in influential U.S. circles, as people seek scapegoats for America's economic and political ills. Anti-free-trade sentiment is gaining hold again, even among policy makers, as backward thinking people want to return to the old days of unchallenged American dominance rather than evolving to ensure continued strength. For instance, the U.S. Senate rejected President Obama's job creation bill in October 2011, but approved one that allows the United States to slap tariffs on Chinese imports. Republican presidential candidate Mitt Romney has taken a particularly strident tone on China, saying it "cheats" the international system by systematically exploiting other economies, stealing intellectual property, and hacking into foreign corporate and government computers.

The real answer of how China's rise will affect the world will be far more nuanced than either camps will admit, and will probably fall somewhere between the dovish and hawkish arguments. The philosophies of these two camps are largely shaped and perpetuated by people with very little on-the-ground knowledge of what China was and what it is becoming. Only rational thinking, based on objective and legitimate data about China, will ensure that corporations and countries properly understand how China's disruptive rise will affect them.

As this book has shown, the End of Cheap China is creating an optimistic consumer class that is poised to fuel revenue growth for those brands that can evolve and cater to their tastes. Companies and countries that can adjust to this new world order—as luxury-brand executives, as well as brands like Nike and Starbucks, have done—will create new jobs and benefit from China's growth. For them, China will likely become one of their largest markets (if not their largest) in the coming decade. They should stop calling China an "emerging market," which underestimates the true power there, and instead view it as a changing market, one equally important as those in the Western world.

On the other hand, free trade and increased trade volume helps the world in the aggregate, but will naturally be painful for those companies and nations unable to evolve along with this new world order or adapt to global competition.

For example, consider what happened to the typewriter industry. Producers went out of business because consumers adopted the personal computer, whose development was driven by Steve Jobs at Apple, among others. Overall, consumers, producers of personal computers, and investors in these companies benefitted from the shift, while for those in the typewriter industry who fought this evolution, the pain was very real. Companies that taught typing realized their days were numbered; those that switched from training people how to use a typewriter to Computers 101 did well, while those unable to make the switch went extinct.

It's understandable that America and other nations being outcompeted by China might grow anxious. But it is important for these countries to suppress the urge to lash out in fear and anger, and concentrate instead on staying ahead of the ensuing changes that will affect them.

A rising power will necessarily disrupt the status quo in political and economic affairs, and some nations and companies will decline, just as the typewriter industry did, or in the way the United Kingdom lost its dominance to America after World War II. This is Darwinism at its starkest.

Italy is a great case study of how a country could benefit from China's rise, but also fall further into economic malaise, depending on how its business community reacts in the next several years. Unless Italy can modernize its production facilities, or convince consumers to pay even higher prices for items put together by Italian master craftspeople, brands like Zegna will shift more production to China, as they have been steadily doing since factories there began moving up the value stream.

Smarter Italian brands will see China's rise as an opportunity rather than a threat. Some might keep manufacturing in Italy for some products, perhaps for more elite, handmade items, but also produce other, more mass-market product lines in China.

One Italian businessman I interviewed saved and even created jobs in Italy by building manufacturing operations in China for a fashion-accessories brand. He kept high-end production in Italy to emphasize brand heritage for marketing purposes, but started producing lower-end products in China. Originally the Italian arm tottered, but the influx of revenue from the cheaper product coming out of China saved the Italian operations. He was able to hire salespeople in Italy to sell the Chinese-made product in Europe, while Chinese customers often demanded the Italian-made products. He was able to take a proactive approach to making money on both sides. His example clearly shows that China's rise can create jobs for evolving companies, rather stealing them as Paul Krugman argues.

One of the dangers bubbling up in the world is that American crusades against free trade are viewed by many in China and other non-Western markets with increasing anger. They believe America's views are unjust and hypocritical. Chinese feel that Americans push for free trade only if it benefits them while being detrimental to China. In their view, Chinese are simply beating the competition, and they find it hypocritical that America is now trying to impose tariffs and other barriers to Chinese trade. Rather than seeing the situation as an undervalued currency granting their advantage, they believe they are winning in the market because they have a more efficient logistics system and workforce than America, and fewer restrictive workforce regulations than countries like France.

They feel that it is China's turn to rise, because so much of America's wealth has been due to Chinese labor. There is palpable anger for America's perceived hypocrisy, a loss of faith in its moral compass in the wake of Guantánamo, and a feeling that America is trying to keep China down. One influential Chinese told me he believes the 2002–2003 SARS epidemic was an "intentional initiative by the Central Intelligence Agency to keep China impoverished." Conspiracy theories aside, the tension between America and China will rise unless calmer heads can prevail, which likely will only happen if economic growth gets back on track.

In the coming years, China's new leaders, especially those promoted during the 2012 leadership transition, will have to appease this current of anger within China. As they try to build and maintain their power base, they will necessarily have to incorporate growing anti-American sentiment within China's military and political establishment, as well as in the general population. But they might not be able to keep as cool a head toward American anti-China rhetoric, as current and previous leaders have done.

As China takes on a larger economic role, will it be able to immediately assume a new global-superpower role and jumpstart the global economy, as those executives in Paris hoped? The reality is that China has far too many internal problems—from lack of affordable housing and medical care, to an educational system that will prevent the country from being innovative—to allow it to be the hoped-for global savior. With so many still living in subhuman conditions like Winnie and Karen, who we met in Chapter 7, the majority of Chinese think the government should save its money by spending it on the nation to protect its own citizens, rather than waste it saving richer people in the developed world.

China should be viewed more as a teenage superpower: displaying glimpses of future genius, but unable to maintain a consistent level of power. Like a teenager, it will need the training and cultivation that college, graduate school, and management training programs offer.

As China evolves, it will offer clues that companies and countries can use to adapt to the new role it plays in world affairs. These clues fall into three key areas:

1. China as a new hegemonic power: One key element in the rise of any superpower is how it will enforce and display its newly acquired power. Will China try to force its ideology on the rest of the world, as most great powers, like the United States, try to do? Does its recent aggressive posturing with its neighbors, like the Philippines in the South China Sea and Japan, foreshadow a return to war, or are China's words and military maneuvers simply a jockeying for power in a new world system, much as kids duke it out on the playground at the start of a school year?

2. Economic growth hitting a wall: Will China's soaring economy ever stall? More and more analysts, even relatively bullish ones, wonder whether its economy can sustain its 10 percent annual growth. They see looming, nonperforming loans in the banking system, and overbuilding in the real estate sector, as indicators that China's growth miracle has stopped. Will this prove to be the case, or will the shift to an economy more reliant on domestic consumption and service industries, and increasing urbanization, bring continued decades of growth? Will improved medical care and social security benefits be enough to convince more Chinese consumers to spend more and save less? If the economic miracle has ended, will the government be able to address

the tension that will undoubtedly arise from frustrated citizens unable to realize their version of the Chinese dream?

3. Reforming the political system: Will China's citizens demand more political rights as they get wealthier, receive their education at foreign universities, and travel to democratic countries, where they will see different ways of life and definitions of human rights? If calls for reform escalate, will the government be able to evolve in a way that grants citizens more rights, or will it shrink from change instead and crack down on any hints of dissent, as Syria has so ruthlessly done? Will an all-out civil war erupt, as in Libya or Yemen, or will the continuing chaos in Egypt, where Coptic Christians worry about the rise of Islamic fundamentalism, prove to Chinese that it is better to coalesce around a single party? Will an evolving political system result in more democratic rights along the Western model, or will China's leadership develop a new form of political system—a one-party, semiauthoritarian one that provides for a diffusion of power and checks and balances?

All of these questions will need to be debated. This book has attempted to answer them by highlighting the Chinese people's optimism and fears, which will influence China's decision makers and force change upon the country. Any change that develops will be consistent with China's needs and historical conditions, rather than repeating what worked in America and the Western world. The country's internal problems will limit its ability and desire to become an ideological, hegemonic power like America—even as it clearly has become an economic one. China will therefore become a very different superpower than the world has previously known—one whose power will be rooted less in an ideological, militant base than in economic growth.

CHINA: THE WORLD'S NEW HEGEMONIC POWER?

As a new superpower, China likely will provide a helping hand whenever possible by taking a greater role in international organizations like the International Monetary Fund and the United Nations, but it will be a very different superpower than the United States has been. Unlike America, it is doubtful that China will try to save the global economy or become the world's policeman. Instead, it will let other nations spend money doing these costly and painstaking things, while they seek out the business opportunities that these actions might produce.

Aside from a culture and ideology that is more focused on internal issues, instead of possessing a missionary-like zeal to convert others to how China thinks, the government still is fearful of internal instability, and will therefore spend most of its time on improving local issues. Moreover, because of strict regulations constraining party officials, government leaders will most likely continue to push their offspring to enter private enterprise to make their money. Most decision making will provide opportunities for well-connected individuals to leverage their relationships to better seize business opportunities.

China's foreign policy will be an offshoot—in many ways, an afterthought—of how it deals with internal issues of stability, and the creation of wealth opportunities for the embedded elite, rather than a cohesive policy designed to shape the rest of the world to emulate China's ideal form of government.

China's laser-like focus on economic growth, and its greater adherence to free trade and capitalism than America's, means China can provide a growth engine for many industries, from agricultural products and medical devices to the luxury sector, among many others. Companies that follow the path of Yum!

Brands, Procter & Gamble, or General Electric by looking to China as their next major growth engine will join in the new Darwinian struggle; either they will evolve and become global winners for the next 50 years, or else they will go extinct.

Yet the country still faces massive challenges—brought about, as this book has shown, by the End of Cheap China—in providing adequate housing, stamping out corruption, ensuring healthy food supplies, and improving the educational system. These problems will not be easily solved, and they will force the government to devote funds and attention to finding answers.

ECONOMIC GROWTH HITTING A WALL

No amount of stimulus or smart planning can offset continued economic pain in the West. There is a very real possibility that a lost decade—or even two—overshadowing entire swaths of the Western world will also severely impact China's growth. Its economy is not completely decoupled from the West, so economic pain there eventually will come to China as exports drop.

Concerns about eurozone debt remain high, as well as worries over a political or even military conflagration if the problem cannot be resolved. Even if more fiscally responsible countries like Germany and Finland try to bail out their neighbors, there are fears that the mounting problems are too large to be solved without defaults, a eurozone breakup, or even worse. Irresponsible bickering in the U.S. Congress has left many Americans angry and hopeless, as unemployment rates have remained above 9 percent despite loose monetary policies and stimulus programs.

In October 2011, hundreds of protesters were arrested in New York during an Occupy Wall Street march, which in its anger mirrored the London riots earlier that year. Their rage was less the product of a concerted, cohesive effort, but instead seemed more to be about frustration over the fact that nothing was getting better for everyday people, while the political and business elite seemed intertwined and corrupt. Similar protests have emerged across the United States.

In the midst of economic turmoil and protests in the Western economies, the balance of power is shifting toward developing countries. Aside from China, India and Brazil are emerging as new economic powerhouses. Yet an ascent to economic dominance is a foregone conclusion for none of these countries. Rampant inflation, red tape, and corruption continue to undermine their governments' legitimacy.

Despite this, worries about an economic and subsequent political collapse in China are greatly overblown. Many analysts, like author James McGregor, argue that the government's legitimacy derives solely from economic growth, and that the country's system will topple if growth does not remain above 8 percent because the people will feel betrayed. That sort of Faustian bargain does not really exist. Rather, the arrangement was more that the government would create peace and stability, stay out of the lives of everyday Chinese as much as possible (unlike the early decades of the Party, when it infiltrated everything), and thus allow business opportunities to develop.

REFORMING THE POLITICAL SYSTEM

Many Westerners assume that continued economic growth and exposure to other cultures will lead middle-class Chinese to want democracy, and that the whole system will collapse if they don't get it. They draw many comparisons to the Arab Spring, which toppled the Mubarak regime in Egypt and Gadhafi's in

Libya. The chief financial officer of one of the world's largest companies asked me, skeptically, "Is the system ready to topple? Do the people support the leadership, and will it be able to accommodate changing wants in China?"

People like that CFO always ask me whether China's government is unchanging, retreating on freedoms, or destined to collapse under the weight of corruption and a political system fraying at the edges. The reality is probably somewhere between the doomsday scenarios and the opinion that the government should never change. China has to continue to evolve politically in order to maintain its robust growth and stability, as Premier Wen Jiabao has repeatedly declared. He has pointed out the need for more transparency and accountability and an end to corruption. The leadership knows continued reform is needed, which is why new regulations are being implemented every day that not only make the country more economically efficient, but that also improve human rights. In 2011, the first capitalist was brought into the Communist Party's Central Committee: Liang Wengen, founder of SANY and one of China's wealthiest men, worth over $9 billion dollars.

Internally, it is doubtful that China will undergo an Arab Spring–like transformation, because the government is making the necessary reforms to ensure the voices of everyday Chinese are better heard. China's population is relatively satisfied with the direction in which the government is taking the country, and there are no major internal forces that are pushing for change. That said, China's government will necessarily have to evolve and reform for its citizens in the coming years, or else more challenges to the growth and happiness of the general population will emerge.

Every year, human rights for average Chinese improve. Their worry, however, is that the good reforms their leaders have put in place since the end of the Cultural Revolution could somehow come to a standstill. The process of improving information flow and transparency within the political system needs to continue. It is likely that the one-party government currently in power will do so.

The End of Cheap China is like a giant wave crashing down on the shoreline with full force. It is fruitless to try to dig in one's heels to withstand the impact of the water, or to hope that life will be exactly the same before the wave came. Companies and people who do so will either get knocked down by the wave, or will remain standing but weakened. The best way to deal with a giant wave is to dive right into it, or jump on a surfboard and ride it all the way to land. Corporations and countries that understand the nuanced changes occurring in China today—and are able to hop on their boards—will have the ride of a lifetime.

EPILOGUE

October 2011

I said good night to a client and walked along Nanjing Road, Shanghai's famed shopping street, where Louis Vuitton and Gap have their flagship stores in China. Glittering lights illuminated the evening skyline as I walked past bustling store after bustling store. Shoppers were in a festive mood, almost as if it were Christmas and the world were not stuck in a global financial crisis, as they toted paper bags brimming with newly bought goodies. The scent of roasting chestnuts wafted to my nose.

An I made my way home, I suddenly was stopped by a woman yelling "Hey, handsome!" at me. I paused and looked at her. Her faced was caked with makeup that seemed to bunch up on the crags lining her face. Unlike that perky young teenager who had knocked on my hotel room door in Changchun, and who easily could have been a cover model for *Teen Vogue*, this woman would fit better in a morticians' magazine as an example of how not to dress. The aged woman told me what 100 bucks would get me and smiled a toothless grin. I shuddered and kept walking.

I glanced backward and saw the woman scurrying away to look for her next mark. China has really changed since that night in the dingy, grubby hotel room in Changchun 13 years before.

——— ACKNOWLEDGMENTS ———

Writing a book is often a solitary experience. Many people helped me figure out what I wanted to say and how to say it.

I must thank my editors at John Wiley & Sons, Inc., Shannon Vargo and Elana Schulman, for excellence in shepherding this project to completion.

I also must thank my colleagues Ben Cavender and James Roy at the China Market Research Group for shouldering more responsibility on client projects and internal operations while I was off writing, and for advising me on how to improve the book. Thanks too should go to CMR summer interns Arielle Sander and Jenny Pang for their help.

Last, I would like to thank my parents, Dad and Deb; my wife, Jessica; and my son, Tom, for their help, support, and love.

INDEX